Dr. Marie Loper, PhD

Dedication

To my clients, first and foremost. Thank you for everything you have taught me over the years. Thank you for inspiring me and this book. Thank you for your patience and caring. Thank you for continuing to show up and do the work, even when it was really hard. If I have failed you in some way, please know that I carry that knowledge with me every day and have done my best to make positive changes for those who followed. I am proud of each of you! It was an honor and privilege to work with you.

To my beta readers: CL, JS, and MT. I could not have done this without you. Writing this after the stroke was one of the hardest things I've ever done and you not only read through multiple drafts, you did exactly what I asked you to do: made this better. You also told me when things sucked exactly as I asked. Like I am a kindergartener holding a pile of poop thinking it is the most awesome rock ever. Y'all rock.

To those of you who actually pay for this? Seriously. Wow. Thank you.

Table Of Contents

Introduction

My name is Marie, and I am a doctoral-level therapist. That means I have my PhD but didn't want to pursue becoming a licensed psychologist (working 4000 hours for someone for free didn't appeal to me). I was in practice for over a decade before I was in an automobile accident that ended my career. I worked predominantly with people who consider themselves (or others consider them) "fringe" – LGBTQIAP+ folx, people who aren't Christian, poly and kinky peeps, and all the rest. The thing I heard from my clients the most often is "You should write a book!" or "You should write a LOT of books!" or "You should write a book, so I don't have to write this down." So, I decided to take their advice and try.

The self-help business is a big business. People spend millions, if not more, every year on books, workbooks, seminars, gurus, life coaches, therapists and more. Why? They want to feel better, and they want to feel better as quickly as possible. Makes sense, right? The problem with that is real, lasting, healing change takes time and often a lot of work. This reality often stops people from even trying.

It was a peculiar feeling—sitting in a therapist's office for the first time. My mind was a whirlwind of skepticism and curiosity, wondering if this path toward self-discovery was filled with clichés or genuine revelations. My anxiety was at an all-time high. Would this person think I was crazy? Would they send me for a grippy-sock-vacation if I said the wrong thing? I'm smart. Surely, I could do this by myself. Right?

But then again, as one of my previous therapists pointed out, if I could do it entirely by myself I would have already.

I vividly recall the awkward silence that enveloped the room, punctuated only by the ticking of the clock on the wall. Was she waiting for me to start? Should I just tell her everything all at once? Why was she staring at me with a slight smile on her face? What were the expectations? It was in the silence in that room, and in others I visited as a client, that I realized therapy was neither a monologue nor a one-size-fits-all solution. It was a conversation—a journey—one that I embarked upon hesitantly but emerged from, enriched and adorned with newfound insights and, unexpectedly, a handful of laughter. What I learned in those rooms informed what I learned in grad school and then subsequent trainings. Combined, they made me a successful therapist.

This book, dear reader, is a tapestry woven from those threads of personal experience, education, trainings, shared wisdom, and more than a slight dash of humor. It's a collection of moments from the therapist's couch where self-discovery met the quirkiness of human existence.

Will reading my book "cure" you? Nope. Is reading my book a substitute for therapy? Absolutely not and I firmly suggest that everyone get into therapy at some point for their own good. With that said, the reality in the U.S. is that many people can't afford mental healthcare. I've been in places in my life where I couldn't. So, I decided to write this book for my clients as well as those of you who are looking for practical advice in how to navigate your current troubles. Think of this as a primer for therapy, or even a companion on your mental health journey.

Therapy—a word that once echoed with stigma—is now a sanctuary where honesty, vulnerability, and growth intertwine. The purpose of this book is simple yet profound: to bridge the gap between the therapeutic journey with the humor that can be found within it.

Within these pages, you'll discover anecdotes, quips, and relatable experiences from therapy sessions—moments that oscillate between introspection and chuckles. The intent is not to diminish the gravity of personal growth but to illuminate it with the lightness of laughter. Through this book, I aim to normalize the therapeutic journey, painting it not as a daunting undertaking but as a shared experience filled with moments of enlightenment, occasional absurdity, and, above all, the beauty of personal growth. Join me as we navigate the labyrinth of therapy, exploring the quirks, clichés, and moments of unexpected hilarity that redefine the path to self-improvement.

There will probably be things in this work that you have heard before, just said in a different way. There may be things here that don't apply to you, so just ignore it. There also might be things that resonate with you that you can then bring to *your* therapist and say "Hey, I want to talk about this!". All of these choices are valid! Read this from start to finish or just focus on the chapters that speak to you the most. You are in charge of your journey, and you get to decide what works best for you.

There are probably going to be healthcare professionals out there who don't agree with a word that I've written. I might even get hate mail for it. I'm okay with that. This is information, advice, and clarification that I have received in my own therapeutic journey as well as evidenced-based treatment approaches that I have shared with my clients over the years. Not everyone agrees with or appreciates my approach to therapy. This book isn't for them. It is for those of you who have questions, who have been trying to get better but can't seem to reach that light at the end of the tunnel, who haven't found that person who can get to the heart of the matter and help you navigate it. If you've ever felt unseen by the mental health world, then this book is for you. I hope it helps you in some way.

After each section I have included a page for any personal notes. There is a workbook that can be purchased separately but is not required but can be helpful. Use the notes' pages to write down epiphanies, questions, anything that you might want to bring up to your therapist later.

Who, What, When, Where, Why, How
Navigating Mental Health Treatment

Healing is a matter of time, but it is sometimes also a matter of opportunity.
-Hippocrates

If you know how to get treatment, skip this section altogether (although you might learn something you didn't know if you keep going)! If you don't, or if you're confused about things, keep on reading. This section is meant to give you information on the types of providers, what they do, and where you can find them.

Types of Providers

I am going to use the terms that occur in the state of Texas. Every state labels their mental health providers differently except for those that are medical in nature. To find out what these providers are called in your state, simply do a Google search on "What are licensed mental health professionals in my state called?". That will tell you what you need to know and what to look for in your area.

For Medication

Psychiatrists

If you need medication, one of the people you want to call is a psychiatrist. They are an MD aka Doctor of Medicine or DO aka Doctor of Osteopathy. You call them "doctor" as a result. These folks have gone to medical school and then, depending on their degree designation, spend a specific amount of time specializing in psychiatry. They are technically the top tier of treatment and as such they are more expensive than their counterparts (if you're paying cash). They also tend to have a waiting list for new patient appointments. Unfortunately, there are more patients than there are doctors, which can mean extended wait times.

The primary difference between a Doctor of Osteopathic Medicine (DO) and a Doctor of Medicine (MD) in psychiatry lies more in their training philosophy rather than their scope of practice within psychiatry itself.

- **Training Philosophy:**

    - *MD (Doctor of Medicine)* primarily practices allopathic medicine. Their training tends to be more focused on the treatment and diagnosis of illnesses through traditional medical approaches.
    - *DO (Doctor of Osteopathic Medicine)* practice osteopathic medicine, which emphasizes a more holistic approach to patient care. Osteopathic physicians are trained to consider the whole person and focus on preventive care

and wellness, in addition to traditional medical treatments.

- **Medical Education:**

  - *MD Training:* MDs attend allopathic medical schools and follow a curriculum based on the principles of traditional medicine, with a strong emphasis on the biological and pharmacological aspects of treatment.
  - *DO Training:* DOs also attend medical schools, but their education incorporates osteopathic manipulative treatment (OMT), which involves hands-on techniques to diagnose, treat, and prevent illness or injury. Additionally, DO training emphasizes a holistic approach, recognizing the interconnectedness of the body systems and the importance of preventive care.

- **Specialization in Psychiatry:**

  - Both MDs and DOs can specialize in psychiatry. The residency training for psychiatry is similar for both types of physicians and typically involves four years of specialized training after completing medical school. During this residency, psychiatrists learn to diagnose, treat, and manage mental health conditions using various therapeutic modalities, including medications and psychotherapy.

- **Board Certification:**

- After completing residency, both MDs and DOs can seek board certification in psychiatry by passing examinations administered by the American Board of Psychiatry and Neurology (ABPN) or other relevant certifying bodies.

In essence, both MDs and DOs can become psychiatrists and offer similar psychiatric services. The primary difference lies in the philosophy and approach to patient care, with DOs often incorporating a more holistic perspective and osteopathic manipulative techniques into their practice. However, in terms of practicing psychiatry and providing mental health care, the distinction between MDs and DOs may not be as pronounced as in other medical specialties.

Psychiatric Nurse Practitioner

A Nurse Practitioner (NPs) can also prescribe medication. They are registered nurses (RN) who have obtained a master's degree and further training in a specified area. For mental health, you will seek out a Psychiatric Nurse Practitioner.

A Psychiatric Nurse Practitioner (PNP) is an advanced practice registered nurse (APRN) who specializes in providing mental health care and psychiatric services. These professionals have received advanced training and education that enables them to diagnose, treat, and manage mental health disorders independently or in collaboration with other healthcare professionals.

Role and Responsibilities:

- *Assessment and Diagnosis:* PNPs conduct comprehensive mental health assessments to evaluate patients' mental and emotional well-being. They assess symptoms, conduct screenings, and diagnose various mental health conditions.

- *Treatment Planning:* Based on their assessment, PNPs develop individualized treatment plans for patients. These plans may include medication management, psychotherapy, counseling, and other therapeutic interventions.

- *Medication Management:* PNPs are authorized to prescribe medications for mental health conditions. They monitor the effects of medications, adjust dosages, and educate patients about the benefits and potential side effects of prescribed medications.

- *Psychotherapy and Counseling:* Some PNPs also provide psychotherapy or counseling services. They offer support, guidance, and evidence-based therapeutic interventions to help patients manage their mental health conditions.

- *Collaboration and Referrals:* PNPs often collaborate with other healthcare professionals, such as psychiatrists, psychologists, social workers, and primary care providers. They may refer patients to specialists or other healthcare providers when necessary.

Scope of Practice:

NPs have a broad scope of practice in providing mental health care. They can work in various settings, including hospitals, psychiatric facilities, community mental health centers, private practices, and primary care settings. Their role is crucial in addressing the increasing demand for mental health services and providing accessible and comprehensive care to individuals with mental health disorders.

In some states (including Texas) NPs prescribe under the supervision of a physician and cannot practice without them. Some will have their own office, and some will be attached to the practice of their supervising physician. There are currently 27 states that allow NPs to practice independently without a supervising physician: Alaska, Arizona, Colorado, Connecticut, Delaware, Hawaii, Idaho, Iowa, Kansas, Maine, Maryland, Massachusetts, Minnesota, Montana, Nebraska, Nevada, New Hampshire, New Mexico, New York, North Dakota, Oregon, Rhode Island, South Dakota, Utah, Vermont, Washington, Wyoming. The other states give NPs varying degrees of autonomy to prescribe medications but only under physician supervision.

Physician's Assistant

Physician's Assistants (PAs) are those who have obtained a master's degree in physician assistant studies. They are trained in the same way that physicians are, but do not attend medical school.

A Psychiatric Physician Assistant (PA) is a healthcare professional who works under the supervision of a licensed psychiatrist or other healthcare providers in the field of mental health. PAs are trained and qualified to perform a wide range of duties within the scope of their practice, including assisting in the diagnosis, treatment, and management of mental health disorders.

Roles and Responsibilities:

- *Assessment and Evaluation:* Psychiatric PAs conduct patient assessments, gather medical histories, and perform mental health evaluations. They assist in diagnosing mental health conditions by evaluating symptoms and conducting preliminary examinations.

- *Treatment Planning:* PAs collaborate with supervising psychiatrists and other healthcare team members to develop treatment plans for patients. These plans may include medication management, therapy, counseling, and other interventions.

- *Medication Management:* Psychiatric PAs assist in prescribing and managing medications for mental health conditions. They monitor patient responses to medications, adjust dosages as necessary, and educate patients on medication use and potential side effects.

- *Therapeutic Interventions:* They may assist in providing therapeutic interventions, such as supportive counseling, psychoeducation, and behavioral therapies under the supervision of a psychiatrist or licensed healthcare provider.

- *Patient Education:* PAs in psychiatry play a role in patient education by providing information about mental health conditions, treatment options, coping strategies, and self-care practices.

- *Collaboration and Referrals:* They work collaboratively with psychiatrists, psychologists, social workers, nurses, and other healthcare professionals to ensure comprehensive care for patients. They may also refer patients to specialists or community resources when necessary.

Scope of Practice:

Psychiatric PAs work in various healthcare settings, including hospitals, psychiatric facilities, community mental health centers, outpatient clinics, and private practices. Their role complements that of psychiatrists and other mental health professionals, allowing for expanded access to mental health services and comprehensive care for individuals with mental health disorders. Only three states allow PAs to practice (including prescribe) independently of a supervising doctor: North Dakota, Wyoming, and Utah. All other states require a varying degree of supervision for PAs. In Texas, PAs are unable to practice independently and are typically found within psychiatrists' offices.

For Therapy

Psychologists

Psychologists are trained professionals specializing in the study of behavior, mental processes, and emotional functioning. They apply their knowledge and expertise in various settings to assess, diagnose, and treat mental health disorders, as well as conduct research, provide therapy, and offer psychological interventions to improve well-being. If you are in need of a "psychological evaluation" you want to visit a psychologist. Psychological evaluations utilize in-depth assessments (including IQ tests) to determine your level of functioning as well as provide specific diagnoses.

Psychologists are referred to as "Doctor", but they are unable to prescribe medications.

Roles and Responsibilities:

- *Assessment and Diagnosis:* Psychologists conduct psychological assessments and evaluations to understand individuals' cognitive, emotional, and behavioral patterns. They diagnose mental health conditions and developmental disorders through various testing and assessment methods.

- *Psychotherapy and Counseling:* Psychologists provide psychotherapy, also known as talk therapy or counseling, to individuals, couples, families, or groups. They utilize evidence-based therapeutic techniques to address emotional struggles, behavioral issues, relationship problems, and mental health disorders.

- *Research and Analysis:* Many psychologists engage in research to study behavior, cognition, emotions, and mental processes. They conduct studies, analyze data, and contribute to advancements in psychological knowledge and understanding.

- *Treatment Planning and Intervention:* Psychologists develop personalized treatment plans for clients based on assessments and diagnoses. They implement therapeutic interventions, behavior modification techniques, and strategies to promote positive changes in clients' lives.

- *Consultation and Collaboration:* Psychologists collaborate with other mental health professionals, such as psychiatrists, social workers, counselors, and medical professionals. They provide consultation, guidance, and expertise in interdisciplinary teams to address complex mental health cases.

Education and Training:

The educational path to becoming a psychologist typically involves the following steps:

- *Bachelor's Degree:* Completion of a bachelor's degree in psychology or a related field, which provides foundational knowledge in psychology.

- *Graduate Education:* Pursuing a doctoral degree (Ph.D. or Psy.D.) in psychology from an accredited program. Doctoral programs involve coursework, research, and practical training in clinical or counseling psychology.

- *Internship and Supervised Experience:* Completion of a supervised internship or practicum as part of the doctoral program, gaining hands-on experience in clinical settings.

- *Licensing and Certification:* Psychologists must obtain state licensure to practice independently. Licensure requirements typically include completing supervised postdoctoral hours and passing a licensing examination. Specialized certifications in various areas of psychology are also available.

Scope of Practice:

Psychologists work in diverse settings, including private practices, hospitals, mental health clinics, schools, universities, research institutions, government agencies, and corporate organizations. They offer a range of services, including assessments, therapy, research, teaching, consulting, and advocacy, contributing significantly to mental health care and understanding human behavior.

Therapists

The term therapist comes from the word psychotherapist. The term psychotherapist is not a title. It is a description of what a person does in this profession. A psychotherapist performs psychotherapy (aka talk therapy). Psychotherapists are mental health professionals trained in providing therapy and psychological interventions to help individuals, couples, families, or groups experiencing emotional or mental health difficulties. They employ various therapeutic techniques to address mental health concerns, promote emotional well-being, and facilitate personal growth.

Roles and Responsibilities:

- *Assessment and Diagnosis:* Psychotherapists conduct comprehensive assessments to understand clients' concerns, emotional struggles, and mental health conditions. They assess symptoms and work towards forming a diagnosis when applicable.

- *Therapeutic Interventions:* They utilize a variety of therapeutic approaches and techniques to help clients address their issues. These may include cognitive-behavioral therapy (CBT), psychodynamic therapy, humanistic therapy, dialectical behavior therapy (DBT), family therapy, and others based on individual needs.

- *Individual or Group Therapy:* Psychotherapists conduct therapy sessions with individuals or groups to explore emotions, thoughts, and behaviors. They provide a safe and supportive environment for clients to express themselves, gain insight, and learn coping skills.

- *Goal Setting and Treatment Planning:* They collaborate with clients to set therapeutic goals and develop personalized treatment plans to address specific concerns or mental health issues.

- *Crisis Intervention:* In certain cases, psychotherapists provide support and intervention during crises or emergencies, aiming to stabilize individuals in distress and connect them with appropriate resources.

- *Education and Support:* Psychotherapists offer education, guidance, and support to help clients understand their conditions, cope with challenges, and develop healthier ways of managing stress and emotions.

Education and Training:

The educational path to becoming a psychotherapist can vary, but it typically includes the following steps:

- *Bachelor's Degree:* Completion of a bachelor's degree in psychology, social work, counseling, or a related field is often the first step.

- *Graduate Education:* Pursuing a master's or doctoral degree in psychology, counseling, social work, or a related field. This may involve a Master of Social Work (MSW), Master of Arts (MA) in Counseling or Psychology, or a Doctor of Psychology (PsyD) or Doctor of Philosophy (Ph.D.) in Psychology.

- *Licensing and Certification:* Psychotherapists typically need to obtain licensure or certification in their respective states or countries. Requirements vary but often involve completing supervised clinical hours, passing examinations, and meeting other criteria set by licensing boards.

Scope of Practice:

Psychotherapists work in various settings, including private practices, mental health clinics, hospitals, schools, community centers, and rehabilitation facilities. They provide counseling and therapy services tailored to the needs of clients dealing with a wide range of mental health issues, relationship problems, trauma, grief, stress, and more. Their goal is to help individuals improve their mental well-being and overall quality of life through therapeutic interventions and support.

There are a number of ways to describe therapists and they depend on the state in which you live. In Texas, licensed therapists are referred to as Licensed Professional Counselors (LPC). Other states label their therapists as Licensed Mental Health Counselor (LMHC), Licensed

Clinical Professional Counselor (LCPC), Licensed Professional Clinical Counselor (LPCC), and Licensed Clinical Mental Health Counselor (LCMHC).

Social Workers

Social workers are professionals who work to improve the well-being and quality of life for individuals, families, groups, and communities. They provide support, advocacy, counseling, and resources to address social issues, mental health concerns, and various challenges people face in their lives.

Roles and Responsibilities:

- *Assessment and Case Management:* Social workers conduct assessments to understand the needs and challenges faced by individuals and families. They develop and implement case management plans to address these needs, connecting clients with appropriate services and resources.

- *Counseling and Support:* Social workers provide counseling, emotional support, and guidance to individuals and families dealing with various issues, such as mental health, substance abuse, domestic violence, homelessness, and more.

- *Advocacy and Empowerment:* Social workers advocate for the rights and interests of their clients. They work to empower individuals and communities, helping them navigate systems, access resources, and exercise their rights.

- *Crisis Intervention:* Social workers provide support and intervention during crises, emergencies, or traumatic events, offering immediate assistance and linking individuals to necessary services.

- *Community Outreach and Education:* Social workers engage in community outreach programs, awareness campaigns, and education initiatives to address social issues, promote mental health awareness, and provide education on various social and health-related topics.

- *Policy Development and Research:* Some social workers engage in policy development, research, and evaluation of social programs and policies to advocate for systemic changes and improvements in social services.

Education and Training:

The educational path to becoming a social worker typically involves the following steps:

- *Bachelor's Degree:* Completion of a bachelor's degree in social work (BSW) or a related field. A BSW provides foundational knowledge in social work principles, ethics, and practice.

- *Master's Degree:* Pursuing a Master of Social Work (MSW) degree from a program accredited by the Council on Social Work Education (CSWE). An MSW provides advanced training in social work practice, research, and specialized areas of social work.

- *Licensing and Certification:* Social workers may need to obtain state licensure or certification, which often involves completing supervised clinical hours and passing a licensure examination. Requirements vary by state and level of practice.

Scope of Practice:

Social workers work in various settings, including hospitals, mental health clinics, schools, child welfare agencies, community organizations, government agencies, private practices, and more. They play a critical role in addressing social injustices, supporting vulnerable populations, and promoting positive change by providing counseling, advocacy, and social services.

Chemical Dependency Counselors

Drug and Alcohol Counselors, also known as substance abuse counselors or addiction counselors, specialize in helping individuals struggling with substance use disorders, alcoholism, and addiction-related issues. They provide counseling, support, education, and guidance to individuals and groups affected by substance abuse.

Roles and Responsibilities:

- *Assessment and Evaluation:* Counselors assess individuals to determine the extent of their substance use and its impact on their lives. They evaluate the severity of addiction, mental health concerns, and other related issues.

- *Treatment Planning:* Drug and Alcohol Counselors develop individualized treatment plans that address the specific needs and goals of clients. These plans may involve therapy, support groups, behavioral interventions, and strategies to overcome addiction.

- *Individual and Group Counseling:* Drug and Alcohol Counselors conduct counseling sessions with clients, either individually or in group settings. These sessions focus on exploring the underlying causes of addiction, coping skills, relapse prevention, and promoting recovery.

- *Education and Support:* Counselors provide education about addiction, its effects, and recovery strategies. They offer guidance on healthy lifestyle changes, coping mechanisms, and resources for clients and their families.

- *Referral and Collaboration:* Substance abuse counselors collaborate with other healthcare professionals, such as psychologists, psychiatrists, social workers, and medical professionals, to ensure comprehensive care. They may also refer clients to other services, such as detox programs or rehabilitation centers, when necessary.

- *Advocacy and Case Management:* Counselors advocate for clients' needs and may assist in accessing resources, housing, employment assistance, and other support services vital to recovery.

Education and Training:

The educational path to becoming a Drug and Alcohol Counselor typically includes the following:

- *Bachelor's Degree:* Some entry-level positions in substance abuse counseling may accept candidates with a bachelor's degree in psychology, counseling, social work, or a related field.

- *Master's Degree or Certification Programs:* Some individuals pursue a master's degree in counseling, social work, or a related field. Others opt for specialized certification programs in substance abuse counseling or addiction studies.

- *Licensing and Certification:* Drug and Alcohol Counselors may need to obtain state licensure or certification, which often involves completing supervised clinical hours and passing a certification examination. Requirements vary by state and country.

Scope of Practice:

Drug and Alcohol Counselors work in various settings, including substance abuse treatment centers, outpatient clinics, hospitals, correctional facilities, and community health centers. They play a crucial role in supporting individuals on their journey to recovery from addiction by providing counseling, support, and resources necessary for achieving and maintaining sobriety. It is important to note that drug and alcohol counselors in most states are prevented from addressing any mental health issues that a person might have that **is not** related to their use. They can only handle substance abuse issues by law. Many psychotherapists are trained to help those with substance abuse issues as well as issues like Bipolar Disorder and trauma. It is important to know the limitations that some of these licenses carry.

Because substance abuse is often considered a separate issue from other mental health issues (and that is how it is billed through insurance), there are different places to look for help than what we've already discussed. I don't think they should be addressed or treated separately but I don't make the rules. If you are seeking mental health treatment already through one of the options already discussed, then please ask for referral sources for substance abuse treatment including drug and alcohol counselors. If you aren't, see below.

- National helplines, such as the Substance Abuse and Mental Health Services Administration (SAMHSA) National Helpline (1-800-662-HELP), provide confidential support, information, and referrals to treatment services in your area.

- Look for reputable addiction treatment centers in your area. Treatment options may include inpatient or outpatient programs, detoxification services, counseling, and support groups.

- Support groups like Alcoholics Anonymous (AA) or Narcotics Anonymous (NA) offer a supportive community of individuals facing similar challenges. If you prefer a secular and non-religious support group, try looking for SMART recovery groups in your area. These groups can be an essential part of the recovery process.

- Addiction specialists or certified addiction counselors have expertise in treating substance use disorders. They can provide tailored treatment plans and therapeutic interventions.

- Local mental health agencies often provide substance abuse treatment services. Contact them to inquire about available programs, counseling services, and support groups.

- Online platforms, such as SAMHSA's Behavioral Health Treatment Services Locator, can help you find treatment facilities, support groups, and counseling services in your area.

- Contact your health insurance provider to understand the coverage for substance abuse treatment services. Many insurance plans cover various aspects of addiction treatment.

- Community-based organizations, religious institutions, and local nonprofits may offer substance abuse support services or be able to guide you to appropriate resources.

Remember that seeking help is a courageous and important step toward recovery. It's crucial to find a treatment approach that suits your individual needs and circumstances. If you or someone you know is in immediate danger or experiencing a crisis, don't hesitate to call emergency services or go to the nearest emergency room.

The Problem with Life Coaches

Many people today are looking for help but are wary of therapy in general. Life coaching offers an opportunity to make significant changes without visiting past traumas, addressing mood disorders, etc. Life coaching has gained popularity as a profession focused on helping individuals achieve personal or professional goals, improve their lives, and navigate transitions. However, like any field, there can be challenges and criticisms associated with life coaching:

- *Lack of Regulation and Standards:* Unlike licensed professions such as psychology or counseling, life coaching lacks standardized regulation. This absence of oversight means that anyone can market themselves as a life coach without specific training or credentials, leading to varying levels of expertise and quality in the field.

- *Varied Quality and Credentials*: With the absence of standardized regulations, the quality-of-life coaches can vary significantly. Some may have relevant training, certifications, or experience, while others may lack formal qualifications or appropriate expertise.

- *Inadequate Training and Competency:* While many life coaches receive training from accredited coaching programs, the quality and depth of these programs can vary. Some coaches may lack sufficient knowledge in mental health, ethics, or specific coaching methodologies.

- *Misalignment with Mental Health Treatment:* Life coaching is distinct from therapy or counseling. While therapists have specific education and training in mental health treatment, life coaches are focused on goal setting, motivation, and accountability. However, some individuals seeking life coaching might require mental health support that surpasses the scope of coaching, and this distinction might not always be clear.

- *Promise of Quick Fixes or Unrealistic Expectations:* Certain life coaches may overpromise or create unrealistic expectations by marketing their services as a quick solution to complex life challenges. Sustainable change often requires time, effort, and a holistic approach.

- *Ethical Concerns:* Some concerns arise regarding ethical boundaries and potential harm when life coaches provide advice or guidance in areas outside their expertise, especially when dealing with sensitive or psychological issues.

- *Financial Exploitation:* High fees charged by certain life coaches, particularly those promising immediate transformations, might exploit vulnerable individuals seeking guidance and improvement in their lives.

- *Lack of Accountability and Follow-up:* Not all life coaches provide structured follow-up or maintain accountability measures, which might hinder the progress of their clients.

It's important to note that many life coaches are dedicated professionals who provide valuable support and guidance to their clients. However, when seeking a life coach, individuals should research their credentials, experience, approach, and client testimonials to ensure they align with their specific needs and goals. Many licensed therapists provide life coaching services in addition to therapy. This isn't to say that there aren't some great life coaches out there who make sure they are doing the right thing for their clients. Just ensure that you are careful about who you choose!

Where to Find Help

Finding mental health help is crucial for anyone struggling with emotional or psychological challenges. Here are some reliable resources to seek assistance. We start with psychiatric hospitals and then move on to outpatient services.

Psychiatric hospitals, also known as mental health or behavioral health hospitals, offer a range of services to individuals experiencing acute mental health crises or severe psychiatric disorders. The specific services provided may vary among hospitals, but here are common psychiatric hospital services:

- **Inpatient Psychiatric Care:** Psychiatric hospitals often admit individuals in acute crisis for intensive stabilization. This may involve close monitoring, medication management, and therapeutic interventions.

- **Psychiatric Assessment and Evaluation:** Mental health professionals conduct thorough assessments to diagnose psychiatric conditions, assess risk factors, and develop treatment plans.

- **Medication Management:** Psychiatrists may prescribe and monitor the use of psychiatric medications to address symptoms and stabilize mental health conditions.

- **Individual and Group Therapy:** Psychiatric hospitals offer various forms of therapy, including individual counseling and group therapy sessions. These sessions focus on addressing specific mental health concerns and developing coping strategies.

- **Crisis Intervention:** Psychiatric hospitals are equipped to respond to mental health emergencies, providing immediate care and crisis intervention for individuals in acute distress.

- **Structured Daily Activities:** Some psychiatric hospitals offer structured daily activities and occupational therapy to help individuals build skills, engage in purposeful activities, and promote overall well-being.

- **Family Therapy and Support:** Involving families in the treatment process is common, and family therapy sessions may be offered to improve communication, understanding, and support.

- **Education and Psychoeducation:** Patients may receive psychoeducation about their mental health condition, treatment options, and strategies for managing symptoms. This can include information on medications, coping skills, and relapse prevention.

- **Discharge Planning:** Psychiatric hospitals engage in discharge planning to ensure a smooth transition back to the community. This may involve referrals to outpatient services, follow-up care, and coordination with community resources.

- **Aftercare and Follow-Up:** Psychiatric hospitals may provide aftercare services or connect individuals with community mental health services for ongoing support after discharge. This typically includes **PHP** (Partial Hospitalization Program) where, after discharging from inpatient hospitalization, you continue mental health programming during the day (or evening) for an extended period of time in a structured format as a step-down to inpatient. **IOP** (Intensive Outpatient) is a further step-down from Inpatient and PHP. It is of significantly shorter duration, usually only a few hours, only a few days a week, which is focused on helping you get back to "real" life from intensive treatment.

It's important to note that psychiatric hospitalization is typically reserved for individuals facing acute mental health crises, and the goal is to stabilize their condition. Long-term mental health care and support are often provided through outpatient services, community mental health centers, and other community-based resources.

- **Therapists and Counselors:**

    - Online Directories: Websites like Psychology Today, GoodTherapy, or TherapyDen allow you to search for therapists by location,

specialization, insurance coverage, and treatment approach.
- Open Path is a non-profit organization that helps those who are underinsured or noninsured obtain therapy services at an affordable rate.
- Referrals: Ask your primary care physician, friends, family, or trusted individuals for therapist recommendations.

- **Mental Health Hotlines and Helplines:**

  - National Suicide Prevention Lifeline: 1-800-273-TALK (8255) provides confidential support for individuals in crisis, including suicidal thoughts or emotional distress.
  - Crisis Text Line: Text "HELLO" to 741741 for immediate crisis support via text messaging.

- **Online Therapy Platforms:**

  - Platforms like BetterHelp, Talkspace, or Pride Counseling offer convenient access to licensed therapists for online counseling.

- **Community Mental Health Centers:**

  - Local mental health centers or community clinics often offer counseling, therapy, and psychiatric services on a sliding fee scale based on income.

- **Employee Assistance Programs (EAP):**

- Many workplaces provide EAP services that offer short-term counseling or referrals to mental health professionals.

- **Support Groups:**

  - Organizations such as NAMI (National Alliance on Mental Illness) offer support groups for individuals and families affected by mental health conditions.

- **Online Resources and Apps:**

  - Mental health apps like Headspace, Calm, or Sanvello offer meditation, relaxation techniques, and tools for managing stress and anxiety.
  - Websites like Mind.org.uk, HelpGuide.org, or the National Institute of Mental Health (NIMH) provide valuable information and resources on various mental health topics.

- **Health Insurance Provider:**

  - Check your health insurance policy for mental health coverage and a list of in-network providers.

- **School or University Counseling Services:**
  - Educational institutions often have counseling centers that provide support to students dealing with academic or personal stressors.

- **Primary Care Physicians:**

- Your primary care doctor can offer guidance, referrals, or prescriptions for mental health concerns and may also collaborate with mental health specialists.

Remember, seeking help is a courageous step towards improved mental health. It's essential to find a qualified professional or support service that fits your specific needs, preferences, and financial situation. Don't hesitate to reach out for help when you need it.

Notes

Therapy 101: The First Session
What to Expect

"The only way out is through."
\- Fritz Perls

Scene: A cozy therapy office. The client, nervously fidgeting, sits across from the therapist.

Therapist: Welcome! So, tell me a bit about yourself.

Client: (Internally) *Hmm, what do I say? Do I start with my childhood pet goldfish or jump straight into my recurring nightmares about clowns?*

Client: (Aloud) Uh, well, I'm a semi-functional adult who occasionally forgets to water plants... and pay bills.

Therapist: (Smiling) Perfect! We'll get along just fine. How do you feel about talking about your feelings?

Client: (Internally) *Feelings? Oh boy, I've compartmentalized those so well, they might as well be in a box labeled "Do Not Open"...*

Client: (Aloud) I've been told I have the emotional range of a teaspoon.

Therapist: Excellent, teaspoons can stir up a lot! How about we start with what brings you here today?

Client: (Internally) *Do I give the dramatic backstory or stick to the abridged version?*

Client: (Aloud) Well, life is a bit like a Netflix series I didn't sign up for... random plot twists, too many characters, and definitely no remote control.

Therapist: (Chuckles) Sounds like a binge-worthy drama series. Let's dive into the pilot episode today.

The session continues with a mix of laughter, nervous ramblings, and the occasional 'aha' moment.

Therapist: Our time is almost up for today. Any takeaways from our chat?

Client: (Internally) *Hmm, is "I need a nap" an appropriate takeaway?*

Client: (Aloud) I think I've discovered that my life's narrative could use some editing for better ratings.

Therapist: (Grinning) Great self-awareness! Remember, you're the protagonist of this story.

Client: (Smirking) Can I get a better wardrobe designer for my character?

The session ends with a promising handshake and a newfound hope for this unexpected therapeutic journey.

When I was an Associate Therapist (called "Intern" back in the day) my license supervisor said something that I have repeated to clients probably thousands of times over the years. (His name is Doug Chan, and he is currently in practice in the Houston area as of the time of this writing if you're interested, by the way).

"If you walk into your kitchen and it's on fire, are you going to look for the source(s) of the blaze while it's on fire or do you put the flames out first?"

Initially, therapy is about putting the fire out. Once that happens, *then* you start looking for the causes and begin to heal it. Starting therapy actually teaches your brain how to handle things differently. Without trying you begin to look at things in a new way. Things don't bother you the same. Sometimes your anxiety, which usually runs wild, isn't that heavy. There is no lightning bolt moment in therapy where you get to go "AHA! There is the healing! I am HEALED!". Instead, it is a gradual realization that things don't suck quite as much as they used to.

The first therapy session is often a mix of nervousness, curiosity, relief, and a whole lot of introductory conversation. Not much "therapy" happens in the first couple of sessions because you and the therapist are getting to know each other. This means that the first few sessions can feel pretty awkward for both of you until you find a rhythm. It is perfectly okay to wait to disclose the serious bits that you need to work on, and some people take this approach. My most stubborn client made me work really hard for two years before they opened up. Others walked into my office and emotionally vomited everywhere because they needed to. That is a valid approach as well. It depends on your level of comfort with the subject matter and yourself. There is no "right way" to do this.

Finding humor in the difficult moments of session can ease the tension and make the process more relatable and enjoyable. Yes, it is okay to laugh in session. When I was a therapist, I tried to make sure that sessions ended with my client laughing, even just a little bit. There were times when clients and I would laugh throughout the entire session. They say, "Laughter is the best medicine" and there is definitely some science there! (But we'll get there later).

Here are some common questions that individuals often have about therapy that are typically addressed in the first session:

- **What is therapy?**

  - Therapy, also known as counseling or psychotherapy, is a professional service provided by trained mental health professionals to help individuals explore their feelings, thoughts, behaviors, and experiences. It aims to improve mental health, manage emotions, and develop coping strategies. It looks like a conversation between two people. It is a unique conversation because during that time the only person who matters in that conversation is you. We talk about anything that you want to talk about. We focus on how you feel about things.

- **How do I know if I need therapy?**

- Only you can decide if you need therapy. You might consider therapy if you're experiencing persistent feelings of sadness, anxiety, stress, or if you're having difficulty coping with life changes, relationships, or traumatic experiences. Therapy can also be beneficial for personal growth and self-improvement. Sometimes therapy is just a place where you can vent about what is happening. Don't have anyone you can vent to? Then maybe you can use therapy.

- **What types of therapy are available?**

  - There are various types of therapy, including cognitive-behavioral therapy (CBT), psychodynamic therapy, humanistic therapy, mindfulness-based therapy, and more. Different approaches suit different needs and preferences. Ask the therapist what their "theoretical orientation" is and what that means for you. They should know how to answer that question. If they don't or can't? Don't work with them.

- **How do I find the right therapist?**

  - Finding the right therapist involves considering factors like their specialization, approach to therapy, location, cost, and your comfort level with them. You can search online directories, ask for referrals, or conduct interviews with potential therapists to find a good fit. In the previous chapter I recommended some resources.

- **How long does therapy take?**

    - The duration of therapy varies depending on individual needs, the type of therapy, and the nature of the issues being addressed. Therapy can be short-term (a few sessions) or long-term (several months or years), depending on the needs, goals, progress and even insurance company requirements if you're using it.

- **Is therapy confidential?**

    - Therapists are bound by federal confidentiality and privacy laws (HIPAA). They cannot disclose information shared during sessions without your consent unless there is a legal obligation or if there's a risk of harm to yourself or others.

- **How much does therapy cost?**

    - The cost of therapy varies based on factors like the therapist's credentials, location, and whether you're using insurance. Some therapists offer sliding-scale fees or accept insurance, while others may charge standard rates. Most therapists advertise their rates on their website or other platform. **It is not offensive to ask a therapist what their rates are and if they offer a sliding scale.** We get that question a lot because cost matters. We are not offended by the question, and we want you to ask if that is a concern for you. Therapists who don't offer a sliding scale want you to be able to find a therapist who does so you can get the help you need.

- **What happens in a therapy session?**

  - Therapy sessions typically involve discussions between you and the therapist about your concerns, feelings, thoughts, and experiences. The therapist may use various techniques, exercises, or interventions based on the chosen therapy approach. They can give you assessments to fill out or even 'homework' to do after session. It all depends on the therapist.

  - At the beginning of your therapy journey, the therapist will likely spend time getting to know you, asking about your background, reasons for seeking therapy, and your goals or expectations from the sessions. Building a trusting and comfortable relationship between you and the therapist is crucial. I practice a lot of self-disclosure with my clients so that they can get to know me and trust me but not all therapists are like that. Not all clients want self-disclosure from their therapist either (and that is perfectly okay).

  - You'll have the opportunity to talk about your current challenges, emotions, experiences, and any issues that brought you to therapy. This discussion may revolve around relationships, work-related stress, mental health symptoms, traumatic experiences, or any aspect of your life causing distress.

- The therapist will listen attentively, asking clarifying questions to understand your perspective and experiences better. They might encourage you to explore your thoughts, feelings, and behaviors, aiming to gain insight into underlying patterns or triggers.

- Based on the therapeutic approach used by the therapist (such as CBT, psychodynamic therapy, mindfulness, etc.), they may introduce specific techniques or exercises. These could include journaling, relaxation techniques, role-playing, mindfulness exercises, or cognitive restructuring to help you address challenges or change unhelpful patterns.

- The therapist will offer feedback, validation, and support as you share your experiences. They may provide insights, alternative perspectives, or challenges to your thinking to foster growth and self-awareness.

- Collaboratively, you and the therapist may set goals for therapy, outlining what you aim to achieve. The therapist might assign homework or suggest exercises to practice between sessions, enhancing the effectiveness of therapy.

- Towards the end of the session, there will be a conclusion where you summarize key points discussed. You might also discuss any emotions that arose during the session or topics you'd like to explore further in future sessions.
- The structure and content of therapy sessions can vary based on the therapist's style, the type of therapy used, and your unique needs. Each session aims to create a safe space for self-exploration, personal growth, and the development of coping strategies to address your concerns.

- **Will therapy work for me?**

  - Therapy effectiveness varies from person to person. Research shows that therapy can be beneficial for many individuals, but its success often depends on factors such as the quality of the therapeutic relationship, your commitment, and the fit between you and the therapist.

- **Do I have to have a mental health diagnosis to go to therapy?**

  - No, you don't need a specific diagnosis to seek therapy. Therapy can be helpful for addressing various life challenges, improving self-awareness, personal growth, and overall well-being, regardless of whether there's a diagnosed mental health condition.

No one really likes to talk about it, but it is time to normalize not having a connection with your therapist. The biggest complaint I heard from my clients while in practice was that people had a lot of bad experiences with therapists for a variety of reasons. Sometimes it's because they felt judged. Sometimes it's because the therapist was a Christian counselor, and they didn't want religion in their session. Sometimes they just couldn't connect because they felt misunderstood. If you find that you're not connecting with your therapist or feel that they're not the right fit for you, it's essential to address this concern. Building a strong therapeutic relationship is crucial for the effectiveness of therapy. I advise people to give a new therapist at least three sessions before walking away. If, after three sessions, you think that things still aren't working, here are steps you can take:

- **Communicate Your Concerns:**

  - If you're comfortable, discuss your feelings openly with your therapist. Be honest about why you feel the fit isn't right and what aspects are causing discomfort or dissatisfaction. This conversation might help improve the dynamic or allow your therapist to make adjustments.

- **Give It Some Time:**

  - Sometimes, it takes a few sessions to develop a rapport or to see if the therapist-client relationship can improve. If you're unsure, consider giving it a couple more sessions to see if things get better. However, **if a therapist ever says anything that causes you concern**

or makes you feel unsafe, end the session and the relationship immediately. I know that finding a therapist can be a long and frustrating journey. With that said, no matter how hard it is to find a therapist in your area, working with the wrong person will do you more damage than good.

- **Request a Change:**

    - If you feel strongly that the fit isn't improving, ask if it's possible to switch therapists within the same practice or organization. Practices should understand the importance of finding the right fit and may facilitate a change.

- **Consider Exploring Different Approaches or Therapists:**

    - If you feel the therapeutic approach isn't suitable for you, consider exploring other therapeutic modalities. Different therapists use varied techniques and approaches, so finding one that aligns with your preferences and needs might be beneficial.

- **Seek Recommendations or Research:**

    - If you decide to look for a new therapist, seek recommendations from friends, family, or healthcare professionals. Online directories, reviews, or therapist-matching platforms can also help in finding potential therapists. If you decide to end a current therapeutic relationship, that therapist should provide you a list of referrals if you ask for them. In many areas, that referral policy is a legal requirement for licensure.

- **Trust Your Instincts:**

  - Trust your instincts and feelings about the therapeutic relationship. Feeling comfortable, heard, and understood is crucial for productive therapy. It's okay to prioritize finding a therapist with whom you feel a better connection.

- **Understand Termination Procedures:**

  - If you decide to end therapy with your current therapist, it's essential to understand their termination procedures. This includes discussing the number of sessions needed before concluding therapy and how to wrap up the therapeutic process. Ultimately, you have every right to not return without discussion.

Remember, finding the right therapist is a personal journey. Your comfort, trust, and the therapeutic alliance are essential components of successful therapy. Don't hesitate to seek a better fit if you feel that your current therapist isn't meeting your needs.

Notes

The Brain
The Science of it All

"The human brain is probably the most mysterious object in the entire universe."
- Isaac Asimov

Emotions involve complex neural processes that are distributed across various areas of the brain rather than being confined to a single location. Multiple brain regions work together to regulate and process emotions, including the limbic system, the prefrontal cortex, and other interconnected structures. Knowing what parts of our brain do 'the things' can sometimes help us to justify our emotional state, even when it's hard to experience. Understanding means coming to a place of knowing that this isn't your fault, it's just how your brain works. Keep in mind that the descriptions below are based on a neurotypical brain. If you have a neuroatypical brain, brain injury, have had a stroke or suffer from some brain diseases, these may not be true for you. Every brain is unique just as every person is. That is part of the reason why therapy and medication work differently with each person.

- **Limbic System:** The limbic system, often considered the primary hub for emotions, includes structures like the amygdala, hippocampus, hypothalamus, and parts of the thalamus. The amygdala, in particular, plays a crucial role in processing emotional responses, particularly fear and threat detection. It is involved in the emotional memory and the regulation of emotional reactions.

- **Prefrontal Cortex:** The prefrontal cortex, especially the ventromedial prefrontal cortex (vmPFC) and orbitofrontal cortex (OFC), plays a role in regulating emotions, decision-making, and social behavior. It's involved in understanding and interpreting emotions, as well as in emotional regulation and impulse control.

- **Insular Cortex:** The insular cortex is associated with various emotional processes, including the experience of empathy, self-awareness, and the subjective feeling of emotions such as disgust, pain, and social emotions.

- **Hippocampus:** While primarily known for its role in memory formation and retrieval, the hippocampus also interacts with emotional processes, especially in the context of emotional memories.

- **Other Brain Structures:** The hypothalamus is involved in regulating the physiological response to emotions, such as heart rate and stress hormone release. The thalamus relays sensory information to the relevant brain areas, contributing to emotional experiences.

Emotions are not localized to specific regions but are the result of complex interactions between these interconnected brain areas. The limbic system, with its various components, is often considered the core of emotional processing, but emotional experiences arise from the integration of signals from multiple brain regions and networks.

The brain's right and left hemispheres both play roles in processing and experiencing emotions, but they do so in somewhat different ways.

Left Hemisphere:

- The left hemisphere of the brain is generally associated with logical thinking, language processing, and analytical reasoning.

- The left hemisphere tends to be more involved in positive emotions such as happiness, and it plays a role in the approach-oriented behaviors linked with those emotions.

- Studies suggest that the left hemisphere is more engaged in the processing of pleasant stimuli and experiences. It might play a part in processing the verbal aspects of emotions, such as labeling and articulating feelings.

- The left hemisphere is more involved in verbal and linguistic processing. While it might not be the primary center for emotional processing, it helps in verbally articulating and labeling emotions related to the traumatic event.

- This hemisphere tends to be involved in more analytical and logical thinking. In the context of trauma, the left hemisphere might be engaged in attempting to make sense of the traumatic experience and integrate it into coherent narratives.

Right Hemisphere:

- The right hemisphere is associated with creativity, spatial awareness, and holistic thinking.

- In terms of emotions, the right hemisphere is more heavily involved in the processing of negative emotions such as fear, sadness, and emotional arousal.

- Research indicates that the right hemisphere plays a crucial role in recognizing emotional expressions in others, understanding non-verbal cues, and interpreting emotions conveyed through facial expressions, tone of voice, and body language.

- This hemisphere is also involved in experiencing and expressing emotions non-verbally, like through prosody (intonation of speech), gestures, and overall emotional tone.

- The right hemisphere is particularly involved in emotional processing and plays a significant role in the initial perception and processing of emotional experiences, especially negative emotions related to trauma, such as fear, sadness, and emotional arousal.

- The right brain is also crucial for processing non-verbal information, such as facial expressions, body language, and environmental cues associated with the traumatic event. Traumatic memories are often stored in a sensory and emotional form in the right hemisphere.

- The right hemisphere is associated with implicit memory, which includes unconscious or automatic recall of experiences. Traumatic memories stored implicitly can contribute to emotional reactions and behaviors triggered by reminders of the trauma.

Prefrontal Cortex:

- Executive Functioning: The prefrontal cortex, particularly the ventromedial prefrontal cortex (vmPFC) and dorsolateral prefrontal cortex (dlPFC), plays a crucial role in regulating emotional responses, impulse control, and decision-making.

- Emotional Regulation: It helps in modulating emotional reactions triggered by traumatic memories. In cases of trauma, the prefrontal cortex may be less activated, affecting the regulation of emotions and responses to stress.

It is essential to note that emotions are complex and arise from the interactions between various brain regions and neural networks. Both hemispheres work together, communicating through the corpus callosum, a bundle of nerve fibers connecting the two hemispheres. While certain emotional processes may be more dominant in one hemisphere than the other, emotions are typically the result of integrated activity across the brain rather than being strictly localized to one side.

Processing trauma involves complex interactions between different brain regions, including the right hemisphere, left hemisphere, and prefrontal cortex, among others.

During trauma processing, the brain attempts to integrate and make sense of the traumatic experience, often involving the interplay between different brain regions. Therapy and trauma-focused interventions aim to facilitate the integration of traumatic memories, regulating emotional responses, and promoting adaptive coping strategies by engaging these brain areas to help individuals heal from the effects of trauma.

Notes

The Therapist's Toolkit
Yes, I'm Going to Mention Journaling

"Therapy is not about 'just talking', it's about finding relief, understanding, and solutions."
-Unknown

Therapists often employ unconventional yet effective techniques to help clients navigate their emotions and thoughts. Therapists often incorporate unconventional tools and exercises to help clients explore their emotions, thoughts, and behaviors in unique ways. These unusual yet effective techniques allow for creative expression and can often lead to profound insights and breakthroughs during therapy sessions. Here are a few (there are hundreds, maybe even thousands of different techniques out there) examples of some unusual but impactful therapy techniques:

Chair Swapping

Therapist: "Let's try an exercise. Imagine you're sitting in my chair. What advice would you give yourself if you were me?"

The Empty Chair Dialogue

Therapist: "Let's invite your inner critic to sit in this empty chair. What would you like to say to it?"

Therapist: "Let's imagine that your (mom/dad/spouse/friend) is sitting in that empty chair. What do you need to say to them?"

The Metaphorical Balloon Release

Therapist: "Write down your worries on these biodegradable balloons. Let's release them and watch them float away."

Painting Your Emotions

Therapist: "Grab a canvas and paint your emotions."

Musical Mood Mapping

Therapist: "Choose a song that resonates with your current emotions. Why that particular song?"

Therapist: "Imagine you can no longer speak and need to tell me who you are. Make a playlist you can share that tells me more about you."

Journaling

You knew I was going to bring it up since it is one of the most recommended tools in a therapist's toolbox. Journaling has been observed to have several psychological benefits, and while individual experiences can vary, there are scientific reasons why journaling is effective:

- **Emotional Release and Processing**: Writing about emotions can help individuals express and release pent-up feelings. This act of emotional disclosure has been linked to reduced stress and improved mood. When people put their emotions into words, it can help them process and make sense of their experiences.

- **Clarity and Problem-Solving**: Writing about challenges, conflicts, or difficult situations may provide clarity and perspective. Journaling encourages self-reflection and can assist in problem-solving by allowing individuals to explore different viewpoints or potential solutions.

- **Stress Reduction**: Studies suggest that expressive writing can reduce stress by lowering cortisol levels (stress hormone). Regularly writing about stressful events or anxieties may help individuals manage their stress more effectively.

- **Enhanced Self-Awareness**: Journaling promotes self-awareness by encouraging individuals to reflect on their thoughts, behaviors, and patterns. This increased self-awareness can lead to a better understanding of oneself, including strengths, weaknesses, and personal values.

- **Improved Mental Health**: Research indicates that consistent journaling may have positive effects on mental health conditions such as depression and anxiety. It can act as a complementary tool alongside therapy or medication by fostering self-reflection and emotional regulation.

- **Boosting Creativity and Cognitive Function:** Some studies suggest that regular writing exercises, such as free-writing or creative writing prompts, can enhance creativity and cognitive processing by engaging different parts of the brain.

- **Tracking Progress and Gratitude:** Journaling allows individuals to track their progress towards goals, acknowledge accomplishments, and express gratitude. Writing about positive experiences or things one is thankful for can enhance feelings of well-being and satisfaction.

- **Physical Health Benefits**: There's some evidence that expressive writing might have physical health benefits, such as improved immune function and better sleep, though more research is needed in this area.

Overall, the act of journaling serves as a tool for introspection, emotional regulation, and cognitive processing. Through written self-expression, individuals can gain insight into their thoughts, feelings, and behaviors, leading to potential improvements in psychological well-being and overall quality of life.

The Art of Self-Reflection

Self-reflection and introspection can be both enlightening and comical, as we navigate the labyrinth of our thoughts and emotions. Injecting humor into these moments can make the process more relatable and enjoyable. Sometimes, therapists will disclose what they learned from their own self-reflection to ease their clients on their journey.

Laughter as Therapy

Laughter holds immense therapeutic value and is frequently used in therapy sessions to create rapport, relieve tension, and foster a positive therapeutic environment. Laughter fosters a sense of connection and resilience, offering a unique way to process emotions and find relief even in difficult moments. Therapists often integrate humor as a valuable tool to promote healing and encourage a hopeful mindset during therapy sessions. If you only discuss the heavy stuff in each session, at a certain point you will dread coming to therapy. At a minimum, that sets you back in the healing process. At a maximum, you could just quit therapy altogether because you are in too much pain. Laughter is just as important in session as crying.

Did you know that the phrase "laughter is the best medicine" has a basis in scientific evidence? Laughter can have positive effects on both physical and mental health. Here are some scientific explanations for why laughter is considered beneficial:

Physical Effects:

- **Stress Reduction**: Laughter triggers the release of endorphins, the body's natural feel-good chemicals. Endorphins promote a sense of well-being and can temporarily relieve pain. It also reduces the production of stress hormones like cortisol, which can contribute to stress reduction.

- **Immune System Boost:** Studies suggest that laughter may enhance the immune system by increasing the production of immune cells and antibodies. This can potentially improve resistance to diseases and infections.

- **Improved Cardiovascular Health:** Laughing can lead to a temporary increase in heart rate and oxygen intake, similar to aerobic exercise. This improved blood flow can benefit cardiovascular health by enhancing circulation and lowering blood pressure.

Psychological Effects:

- **Mood Enhancement:** Laughing stimulates the brain's reward system, leading to improved mood, increased happiness, and a sense of relaxation. It can alleviate symptoms of anxiety and depression by promoting a more positive outlook.

- **Social Bonding and Connection:** Laughter is often a social activity that fosters connections and strengthens relationships. Shared laughter can enhance social interactions, improve communication, and create a sense of belonging and unity among individuals.

Cognitive Effects:

- **Enhanced Cognitive Function:** Laughing can stimulate mental function by increasing alertness, creativity, and problem-solving abilities. It can help reduce mental fatigue and improve overall cognitive performance.

Pain Reduction:

- **Pain Modulation:** Laughter can temporarily alleviate pain by stimulating the release of endorphins, which act as natural painkillers. It can also distract from discomfort, reducing the perception of pain.

Incorporating humor and laughter into daily life can contribute positively to overall well-being and complement other health practices. Ultimately, laughter's positive effects on physical, emotional, and social aspects of health make it a valuable and enjoyable aspect of a healthy lifestyle. This is not an exhaustive list of techniques, but they are ones that I personally have seen work while in session. And, because I am a therapist, I had to push journalling too. You'll thank me later.

Notes

That One Piece of Advice
Was it Something I Said?

The greatest discovery of any generation is that human beings can alter their lives by altering their attitudes of mind.
- William James

There are things that people say to us, in passing or in intense moments, that make such a deep impression that we can never forget them. This section can be used in conjunction with the workbook that accompanies this work. You don't need to, there is no pressure. The workbook is a way to help you process the following statements either on your own or with your therapist. The advice is the same regardless of whether you use the workbook or not. I've broken down the advice by topic (and the pieces of advice will be in bold) so that you can find the ones you believe you're in need of and skip the ones that don't resonate. There are a number of mood disorders and mental illnesses that could have been addressed here, but I do not discuss them in this book. That would create a really big book that would be hard to get through (but maybe I'll write another one someday). Instead of doing that, I addressed the two things that the majority of disorders have in common: anxiety and depression. Keep that in mind as you look through the advice on handling these topics. Sometimes, all it takes is one piece of advice to change your entire perspective.

Fear

Before we discuss anxiety, it is important to address what the underlying cause of all anxiety is: fear. Fear is a fundamental human emotion that serves as a natural response to perceived threats or dangers. It's an adaptive mechanism that has evolved over time to help protect us from harm and ensure our survival. Several factors contribute to why we experience fear:

- **Survival Instinct**: Fear is deeply rooted in our evolutionary history. Throughout human evolution, those who were more cautious and alert to potential dangers were more likely to survive and pass on their genes. Fear is encoded in our DNA as a survival mechanism. It used to be very, very necessary in order to keep us alive. The problem is that we now have very few things we need to fear for our survival. That means that fear doesn't have a job to do any longer. **Fear has nothing to protect you from.** Without a job to do, fear looks for ways it can be useful. In some people that means you now become afraid of everything. Including happiness.

- **Protection Mechanism**: When faced with a perceived threat, whether it's physical, psychological, or emotional, fear prompts a series of physiological changes in the body. Hormones like adrenaline and cortisol are released, increasing heart rate, sharpening focus, and redirecting energy to essential functions, preparing us to respond to the threat. This is what we refer to as the body's fight-flight-freeze-fawn response, preparing us to either confront the threat, flee from it, freeze in terror to make the threat pass us by, or fawn all over the person who is causing the threat to get them to stop.

- **Learned Responses:** Fear can also be learned through experiences. For instance, if someone has a negative or traumatic experience associated with a specific situation, object, or event, they may develop a fear response when encountering similar circumstances in the future. Those experiences become wounds. Those wounds increase fear. Think of it this way: **Fear is a guard dog standing watch over your wounds. All it wants to do is protect you. When someone gets too close to a wound that dog goes into overdrive screaming, barking, lunging, and snapping.**

- **Cognitive Appraisal:** How we perceive and interpret situations plays a significant role in experiencing fear. Factors like uncertainty, unpredictability, and lack of control can contribute to feelings of fear and anxiety. When the fear of those factors gets out of control, **Fear becomes your only companion.** Fear is isolating and keeps you from being able to live.

- **Cultural and Social Influences:** Cultural norms, societal expectations, and learned behaviors from family and peers can shape our fears. Some fears may be culturally specific or influenced by social conditioning. If your caregivers were afraid of something, chances are they passed that fear down to you.

While fear is a natural and often protective response, it can also become problematic when it is excessive or persistent, leading to anxiety disorders or phobias. Understanding and managing fear involves recognizing when it's beneficial (in situations where danger is real) and when it may be irrational or excessive, requiring intervention or support to address its impact on daily life. Techniques like exposure therapy, mindfulness, and cognitive-behavioral approaches can help individuals manage and overcome irrational fears or phobias.

Anxiety

Anxiety is Fear's attempt to protect you. While stress can contribute to feelings of anxiety, the relationship between stress and anxiety is not always straightforward. **Anxiety is your brain interpreting your stress as a threat.** That flat tire? Your brain thinks it is a threat. Being late to work? Same thing. Hang nail? Still a threat (although a very tiny threat).

Anxiety can be described as a state of heightened worry, apprehension, or fear in response to perceived threats or challenges. When faced with stressors, whether they are real or perceived, the brain and body react by triggering the release of stress hormones like cortisol and adrenaline. These hormones prepare the body for a flight-fight-freeze-fawn response, which is a natural survival mechanism designed to help deal with immediate danger.

In some cases, when stress becomes overwhelming or prolonged, the brain may interpret these stressors as threats, leading to a chronic state of anxiety. This perception of stress as a constant threat can contribute to the development or exacerbation of anxiety disorders.

However, it's essential to note that anxiety can stem from various sources, including biological, genetic, environmental, and psychological factors. Not all stress leads to anxiety, and not everyone responds to stress in the same way. While stress can certainly contribute to feelings of anxiety, the relationship between the two is intricate and can vary from person to person.

Therapeutic techniques, such as mindfulness, cognitive-behavioral therapy (CBT), and stress management strategies, can be helpful in addressing both stress and anxiety by teaching individuals how to better cope with stressors and manage their responses to them.

The main issue is that **Anxiety is a liar**. The voice of fear sounds like you in your own head because it has been in there for so long. That voice is made up of the messages family, friends, peers, society, culture, etc. gave you, all combined to remind you of all the things you should be afraid of. This voice is very similar to the ones tied to depression and self-esteem (which we'll get to later). The main two things that every person with anxiety has in common is that they spend all of their time and mental energy either reliving the past or anticipating the things in the future that could be bad. It is exhausting because there are just so many things to be afraid of. **Fear wastes time** but telling someone "There's nothing to worry about!" isn't helpful. It doesn't matter what *you* think when *their fear* is so overwhelming.

One of the things that I told clients frequently was **Don't borrow trouble**. Don't reach into the future and worry about something that might happen but hasn't yet. If you do, then you're literally borrowing something from the future to worry about it now. Future focused anxiety means you are afraid of all the things that *could* go wrong. The emphasis is on "could" instead of "is". Logically we know that the future hasn't happened yet or else it would be the present. If it hasn't happened yet, why is your focus there? Anxiety convinces us that if we worry about it, then we are prepared for it, and if we are prepared for it, we can then handle it better. Unfortunately, that isn't true and never will be. First, we can only anticipate what might happen (unless you're psychic). We never really know exactly what is going to occur. Second, being afraid of it doesn't stop it from happening. Finally, if the thing that you're worried about actually does happen, and you worried about it until it did, *you put yourself through that twice.* Instead of dealing with whatever happens when it happens, we torture ourselves first. Doesn't sound like a good time, does it?

Past focused anxiety relives painful memories over and over while we focus on what we "should have", "could have", or "would have" done differently. **Shoulda, woulda, and coulda are the three most dangerous terms in the English language**. They create guilt, shame, and remorse but not healing. The most important thing to remember about past hurts is that they are in the past, done, completed, over. You know this logically but your feelings about it are different. It feels like you need to keep going over all of the ways you've screwed up over and over. One of the things you've probably heard from somewhere, that I've said multiple times, is that **Feelings are not facts.** At their most basic, feelings are a chemical reaction to a stimulus. But just because you experience them, does not mean that how you feel becomes a fact. Too many people confuse the two. **How you feel is always valid (because it is your emotional reaction) but it isn't always true.** Self-forgiveness is how you stop the guilt, shame, remorse, and be able to leave your past in the past where it belongs. We'll get to self-forgiveness later in the book, but for now let's return our focus to anxiety.

Anxiety is something we feel but it also affects how you think about things and how often. Anxiety can often lead to overthinking. When someone experiences anxiety, they might find themselves excessively worrying about past events, future possibilities, or potential outcomes. Overthinking is a common response to anxiety, and it involves dwelling on negative thoughts or uncertainties to an extent that can be overwhelming and interfere with daily life.

Here are some ways anxiety can contribute to overthinking:

- Anxiety can cause individuals to repeatedly dwell on distressing thoughts, events, or feelings. This constant dwelling on negative aspects can perpetuate feelings of anxiety and contribute to a cycle of overthinking.

- Anxiety can make someone more prone to catastrophizing, where they tend to magnify or exaggerate the significance of potential negative outcomes. This can lead to a heightened sense of worry and overthinking about worst-case scenarios.

- Individuals experiencing anxiety might fixate on achieving perfection or avoiding mistakes, leading to overthinking situations as they try to anticipate every possible outcome or flaw.

- Anxiety can make it challenging for individuals to let go of worries, causing them to revisit and overanalyze situations repeatedly.

- Constant vigilance due to anxiety can lead to overthinking as the mind remains on high alert, continuously assessing and reassessing situations for potential threats.

Managing anxiety-related overthinking often involves strategies to address the underlying anxiety itself. Practicing mindfulness and relaxation exercises can help individuals ground themselves in the present moment and reduce the tendency to overthink. While therapy, particularly cognitive-behavioral therapy (CBT), can help individuals identify and challenge negative thought patterns that contribute to overthinking. Establishing boundaries around excessive worrying or allocating specific time for problem-solving can prevent overthinking from dominating all aspects of life. Talking to a therapist, counselor, or trusted individual can provide perspective and support in managing anxiety and overthinking.

Recognizing the connection between anxiety and overthinking is an important step in finding effective strategies to cope with both. Combining self-awareness with appropriate coping mechanisms can help individuals regain control over their thoughts and reduce the impact of overthinking on their well-being.

Depression

Depression is a multifaceted mental health condition characterized by persistent feelings of sadness, loss of interest or pleasure in activities, changes in appetite or sleep patterns, low energy, difficulty concentrating, feelings of worthlessness or guilt, and, in severe cases, thoughts of self-harm or suicide. It can affect how a person thinks, feels, and behaves, often interfering with their ability to function in daily life.

Several factors contribute to the development of depression, including:

- **Biological Factors:** Imbalances in brain chemistry, genetics, hormonal changes, and alterations in neurotransmitter levels (such as serotonin, dopamine, and norepinephrine) can play a role in the onset of depression.

- **Psychological Factors:** Certain psychological vulnerabilities, such as a history of trauma, chronic stress, low self-esteem, or personality traits, can increase the risk of developing depression.

- **Environmental Factors:** Stressful life events, such as loss, relationship problems, financial difficulties, or major life changes, can trigger or contribute to depression. Additionally, ongoing exposure to adversity or adverse living conditions can impact mental health.

- **Medical Conditions**: Certain medical conditions or chronic illnesses, such as chronic pain, thyroid disorders, or neurological conditions, can be linked to depression.

Depression is not just feeling sad or having "the blues." It is also not "just a phase" for your teenager. It is a serious mental health condition that can vary in severity and duration. There are several types of depression, including major depressive disorder (MDD), persistent depressive disorder (dysthymia), bipolar disorder, seasonal affective disorder (SAD), postpartum depression, and others. There is situational depression, where your depression starts with a specific event (like losing a loved one) and then ends as you begin to feel better. Clinical depression does not have a specific starting event, nor does it end in a reasonable amount of time without treatment.

Treatment for depression often involves a combination of approaches tailored to an individual's needs, which may include psychotherapy (such as cognitive-behavioral therapy or interpersonal therapy), positive coping skills, medication (like antidepressants), lifestyle changes (exercise, a healthy diet, stress reduction), and support groups or peer support. Combining more than one approach has the highest likelihood of success.

It's crucial for individuals experiencing symptoms of depression to seek professional help from mental health practitioners, such as therapists, counselors, or psychiatrists, as early intervention and appropriate treatment can significantly improve outcomes and help manage the condition effectively. You can manage it effectively, by the way. Your depression will tell you all sorts of things that are untrue because **Depression is a Liar.** Just like with anxiety, the voice of depression sounds like you in your own head because it has been in there for so long. That voice tells you the most horrible things. "You're worthless" it whispers in your ear. "No one would notice if you were gone" or "They'd all be better off without you" are favorites in the depression script. As is "Nothing can help you. Not therapy or medication. Nothing." It is almost as if you've been possessed by a demon that is trying to kill you. Because depression's aim *is* to kill you. That's why you are exhausted no matter how much you sleep. That's why you don't have the energy to shower or eat or clean. Sometimes, having depression bad enough means that your coping skills take too much energy to work. What is left is then suicidal thoughts which can, if around long enough, even become what therapists refer to as a maladaptive coping skill.

Suicidal thoughts (also called ideation) are divided into two categories: passive and active. Passive suicidal ideation refers to not wanting to be alive but not having a plan. Passive suicidal thoughts are similar to "I'm not suicidal but I wouldn't mind being hit by a bus". There is no plan and you do not see yourself actually committing suicide. You just aren't going to do anything to take care of yourself or avoid harm. People with passive suicidal thoughts have success with therapy and medication. Active suicidal ideation is the exact opposite: there is the motivation, the means, and the plan to unalive yourself. People with active suicidal thoughts need to seek crisis treatment immediately. Crisis treatment includes inpatient hospitalization and outpatient services where a person is heavily monitored until the thoughts go away.

Self-Harm

When discussing depression and suicide, you must discuss self-harm. Especially because there is a link between depression and self-harm. Self-harm refers to intentionally inflicting injury or damage to one's body without the intent of suicide. It's a complex behavior often associated with emotional distress, psychological pain, or the attempt to cope with overwhelming feelings or thoughts. Self-harm can take various forms that I won't be discussing here to avoid triggering anyone but also to not give anyone new ideas on how they can hurt themselves.

It's essential to understand that self-harm is not a healthy or effective way to cope with emotional pain or stress. It isn't a suicide attempt, and it won't necessarily turn into one either. However, it is dangerous both physically and emotionally. It's a sign of significant emotional distress and should be taken seriously. While self-harm might provide temporary relief or a sense of control to some individuals, it doesn't address the underlying issues causing distress and can lead to further physical and emotional harm.

Several reasons may contribute to someone engaging in self-harming behaviors:

- **Coping Mechanism:** Individuals might use self-harm as a way to cope with overwhelming emotions or to numb emotional pain temporarily.

- **Communication of Distress:** Some people may use self-harm as a way to express their emotions or communicate their inner struggles when they find it challenging to verbalize their feelings.

- **Sense of Control:** Engaging in self-harm can create a temporary sense of control or relief from emotional turmoil for some individuals.

- **Trauma or Mental Health Issues:** Self-harm can be linked to trauma, depression, anxiety, borderline personality disorder, or other mental health conditions. It may serve as a maladaptive way to manage symptoms.

If you or someone you know is engaging in self-harm, seeking help is crucial. It's essential to address the underlying causes and obtain appropriate support. I have not listed potential coping skills here because self-harm needs to be dealt with in therapy **without exception**. You may be able to quit self-harming without help or by using tracking apps and such. Unfortunately, without outside help, the reason(s) for self-harm still haven't been dealt with, which will cause a relapse at some point.

Notes

Boundaries
The Art of Saying No

"Good fences make good neighbors"
-Robert Frost

That's quite a jump to a new topic, huh? Except, it isn't really. People who have depression and anxiety (as well as trauma or other mental disorders) frequently struggle with boundaries, which is why they are a necessary part of positive mental health. This is one of the most heavily discussed topics in therapy. People with poor boundaries often become door mats for people or even a human emotional support animal. If you grew up in a home where you were parentified, you weren't allowed to say no. If one or both of your parents were abusive, you weren't allowed to say no. If a caregiver was a narcissist, you weren't allowed to say no and *you were supposed to emotionally regulate them instead of yourself.* Take this example. It is a combination of things I have heard over the years in session.

Growing up with your mom was volatile. She was emotionally manipulative and abusive, but you didn't understand that at first. You just figured out quickly how to make her stop when she got out of control. Because if you didn't, things would get

What we have here is a boat-rocking scenario. Your family is on this one boat. It is crowded from front to back and side to side. You're smooshed in like sardines and the boat sits low enough from the weight of all those people that water sloshes over the sides if you're not careful. You are very, very careful. But every so often, your mom stands straight up in the boat and then jumps up and down. Everyone is panicking, screaming except your mom who is still having her temper tantrum, oblivious to the water pouring into the boat. You rush in to soothe her, as you've been trained to do, getting her calm and seated, before you return to your seat. Sometimes you don't want to soothe her. You're tired. But whenever you try not to, when you ask for someone else to do it, the rest of the family turns on you, forcing you to keep her from rocking the boat. The cycle continues, uninterrupted, until you realize that the boat is sitting in only knee-high water. No one before you bothered to see if you were ever really in danger, they just assumed they were. Want to stop being trapped in the cycle? Get out of the boat. That is easier for me to say than for you to do and I understand that. Keep reading.

Several factors contribute to why individuals might struggle with establishing or maintaining healthy boundaries:

- **Upbringing and Environment**: The environment in which individuals are raised can significantly influence their ability to set boundaries. In some families or cultures, boundaries might not be emphasized or respected, leading individuals to struggle with establishing their own boundaries as adults.

- **Fear of Rejection or Conflict:** Some individuals avoid setting boundaries because they fear it might lead to conflict or rejection. They prioritize maintaining relationships or avoiding confrontation over their own needs and well-being.

- **Low Self-Esteem or Insecurity:** People with low self-esteem may struggle to assert their needs or set boundaries because they feel undeserving, or fear being seen as selfish.

- **Desire for Approval:** Seeking validation or approval from others can lead individuals to ignore their own boundaries in an attempt to please others or gain acceptance.

- **Past Trauma or Abuse:** Individuals who have experienced trauma or abuse may have difficulty establishing boundaries due to past experiences where their boundaries were violated. This can lead to confusion about what healthy boundaries look like and difficulty asserting them.

- **Lack of Awareness or Assertiveness Skills:** Some individuals might not have been taught or developed the necessary skills for setting and maintaining boundaries. They may lack awareness of their own needs or struggle with assertive communication.

- **Cultural or Societal Expectations:** Cultural norms or societal pressures may discourage setting boundaries, emphasizing self-sacrifice, or putting others' needs above one's own.

It's important to note that the reasons for lacking boundaries can vary widely among individuals, and multiple factors can contribute simultaneously. It does not say anything negative about you. You haven't done anything wrong. You're just doing your best and saying no can be scary. Developing healthy boundaries often involves self-reflection, self-awareness, and learning new skills. Therapy or counseling can be beneficial in understanding boundary issues, building self-esteem, learning assertiveness skills, and establishing healthier patterns in relationships. With time, practice, and support, individuals can learn to set and maintain boundaries that prioritize their well-being while fostering healthy connections with others.

Healthy boundaries are the key to a healthy relationship with self and others. Unhealthy ones contribute to unhealthy (and even abusive) relationships as well as being taken advantage of. Boundaries refer to the personal limits and guidelines that individuals set to establish their emotional, physical, and mental well-being. They are not meant to control other people, only protect yourself from their behavior(s). Boundaries define how individuals interact with others, handle relationships, and protect themselves from being manipulated or mistreated. Healthy boundaries are an essential aspect of self-care and fostering healthy relationships. In fact, **Boundaries teach others how to love us**. If they argue with your boundaries, it is because they mean to stomp them. People who understand the value of boundaries will thank you for helping them love you in a healthy way.

Here are different types of boundaries:

- **Physical:** These boundaries relate to personal space, touch, and physical interactions. For instance, some individuals might be uncomfortable with certain types of physical contact and establish boundaries accordingly.

- **Emotional:** Emotional boundaries involve setting limits on how much emotional energy, thoughts, and feelings one shares with others. This includes protecting oneself from emotional manipulation or allowing oneself to express emotions in a safe and healthy manner.

- **Mental:** Mental boundaries involve protecting one's thoughts, beliefs, and opinions. It's about respecting differences in perspectives and not allowing others to impose their thoughts or beliefs onto oneself forcefully.

- **Time:** Time boundaries involve managing one's time and commitments. It includes setting limits on how much time one spends on work, relationships, social activities, and personal pursuits.

Establishing and maintaining healthy boundaries is crucial for several reasons:

- **Self-Respect:** Boundaries show self-respect and self-worth by honoring one's needs and values.

- **Healthy Relationships:** Healthy boundaries are fundamental for fostering positive relationships. They help in maintaining mutual respect, understanding, and empathy.

- **Self-Care:** Setting boundaries is an act of self-care that promotes emotional well-being and reduces stress.

Tips for setting healthy boundaries:

- **Self-awareness:** Understand your own needs, values, and comfort levels to define your boundaries effectively.

- **Communication:** Clearly communicate your boundaries to others in a respectful and assertive manner.

- **Consistency:** Maintain consistency in upholding your boundaries. Be firm in your limits while respecting others' boundaries as well.

- **Self-Advocacy:** Advocate for yourself and don't feel guilty for setting boundaries that prioritize your well-being.

Remember, setting boundaries doesn't mean shutting people out or being rigid. It's about creating a healthy balance that respects your needs and values while fostering positive and respectful relationships with others. Boundaries can also be influenced by the other person's behaviors. Sometimes rigid boundaries are necessary with someone who has harmed you in the past and may do so in the future. The important thing is to **Trust your gut.** Your heart can lead you astray, your mind can talk you out of it, so your instincts, which will never lead you wrong, need to be paid attention to. There are a lot of people out there who are willing and able to manipulate to get their needs met. That is why you need to train yourself to pay attention to people's behaviors, more than what they say. Given enough time, everyone will show you who they really are. Which brings us to our next piece of advice: **When someone shows you who they are, believe them.**

What does that have to do with boundaries? A lot, actually. Our boundaries change and evolve depending on who we are interacting with. People we don't like will require stricter boundaries. People we love have fewer. When you first meet someone, they are typically on their best behavior. This includes people who plan to take advantage or harm you. When you want to see the best in people you can be led astray. This is not to say that you shouldn't seek out the best in people. It just means that while you are doing so, you need to be able to be realistic as well. Paying attention to, and being realistic about, another person's behavior only saves you heartache.

You don't owe anyone anything (unless you have children), and that includes an explanation. If you want to, then say no to whatever it is that you want to say no to. I know that is a hard thing to imagine, isn't it? You probably have the beginnings of a panic attack just thinking about it. First, breathe. Gentle breaths. Now repeat after me. **No is a complete sentence.** Good. Now again. Keep this mantra in mind whenever you are faced with a decision. And start small. Ask a friend or loved one to help you practice saying no. Have them start by asking you silly questions that you can easily say no to. "Can I set your car on fire?" or "Can I pour glue into your shampoo?" are examples of questions that should be pretty easy to say no to. Do that as often as you can to practice your no. When you're comfortable saying no to the easy stuff, up the ante bit by bit until you feel like you're ready to do it on a regular basis. Practice makes perfect, even in therapy.

Once you're comfortable with your no, we need to practice how to deliver it. When someone doesn't want you to have boundaries, they will seek out any opportunity to try to force their way through them. You might feel the need to explain or justify your no. Don't do that. Don't **JADE** (**J**ustify, **A**rgue, **D**efend, **E**xplain). And here is why:

- **Justify** – Don't justify your decision. They will have an argument ready and waiting. They want your attention and will do anything to get it. The longer you talk, the more likely you will give in.

- **Argue** – Arguing with someone who won't take no for an answer, is a recipe for disaster. You cannot win. They will always be better at arguing than you are because they are used to bullying people into agreement. They are the master in this scenario, and you are so used to giving in, you can't even think effectively.

- **Defend** – There is no need to defend your decision. You don't owe them anything, remember? You are not trying to convince them, because you can't. The only way you can is if you do what they want you to do.

- **Explain** – Here's the trickiest one for most people. We try to explain ourselves because we believe internally that *if I just use the right words, I can convince them to believe me and stop their behavior.* That is a very logical assumption and would absolutely work if you were dealing with someone who didn't have the emotional range of a turnip.

The thing to remember about JADE is that abusers, boundary stompers, and narcissists (oh my!) are counting on you trying to convince them through justification, arguing, defending yourself, and even explaining. To convince someone of something, they have to be willing to be convinced. They have to be willing to see things from your perspective, which they are unwilling to do at a minimum and incapable of doing at maximum. When you stop trying, they stop being able to get an emotional reaction from you and your boundaries are safe.

Remember how I said earlier that you don't owe anyone anything (unless you have children)? And that no is a complete sentence? JADE is a continuation of that. When you use your no without remorse, when you cannot be tricked into JADE, you now no longer put up with people and their manipulations/boundary stomping/abuse/etc. Sounds easy in theory but it is definitely harder in practice. The first step is recognizing the types of people you need boundaries with. Who in your life needs to be told no? What if you can't recognize them? What if you're so used to saying yes that you have no idea what requests or issues are even reasonable?

Enter **The Three F's**. Now, if the f-word bothers you, this is your warning that you're going to see it a bit in the next section so prepare yourself. Otherwise, read on.

The Three F's stand for – Feeding me, Financing me, and/or Fucking me. As in, if the person who you are struggling does *not* meet Three F's then it is a lot easier to say no. Why would you bother saying yes to someone who doesn't? While it is crude, the saying is meant to remind you that just because someone is in your life does not mean that they are entitled to anything from you. You don't have to play their game(s). You can give yourself permission to disengage from them. I tell clients that a person better meet two out of three of the F's before you even consider anything other than a "no" (and the Feeding means groceries in my fridge, not buying me dinner). By the way, the "fucking" of the F's doesn't just represent sex. It represents intimacy on an emotional and psychological level as well as the physical. You deserve to have your wants, needs, and desires met just as much as anyone else. You deserve to pick the people who can do that and not have anything to do with those people who can't or won't.

Now that you have started to choose people who will respect your boundaries and have been practicing your "no", we come to the next piece of advice in your journey with boundaries. Let's say that you are standing in front of a person and that person is repeatedly punching you in the face. You say "NO!" repeatedly after laying down a boundary: "I don't want to be hit! Stop!". Yet, the person just keeps punching you no matter what you say. Why is that when you've technically done everything right? It's because **Boundaries without consequences are useless.** Instead of just saying no the next time they punch you, you say stop and then punch them back. All of a sudden, they've stopped punching you because there is now a consequence to their behavior.

Boundaries without consequences lack the necessary reinforcement to maintain their effectiveness. Establishing boundaries is a crucial aspect of self-care and healthy relationships, but for boundaries to be respected and taken seriously, they need to have consequences when crossed or violated.

When setting boundaries, it's essential to communicate not just the limits but also the consequences of disregarding those boundaries. Consequences provides accountability and help reinforce the importance of respecting personal limits. They serve as a deterrent against boundary violations and emphasize the significance of maintaining mutual respect in relationships.

Here are a few reasons why boundaries without consequences may be ineffective:

- **Lack of Clarity:** Without clear consequences, the seriousness of the boundary might be unclear, leading others to dismiss or test the boundary.

- **Diminished Impact:** Boundaries without consequences may be perceived as mere suggestions rather than non-negotiable limits, making them more likely to be ignored or violated.

- **Boundary Testing:** Without consequences, individuals might repeatedly test the boundaries, assuming there will be no repercussions for overstepping them.

- **Undermines Self-Respect:** Not enforcing consequences for boundary violations can undermine one's self-respect and make it challenging to maintain healthy relationships based on mutual respect.

When establishing consequences for boundaries, it's important to consider:

- **Clarity:** Clearly communicate the consequences in a calm and assertive manner when discussing the boundaries.

- **Consistency:** Be consistent in upholding consequences when boundaries are disregarded. Inconsistency can weaken the boundary and undermine its effectiveness.

- **Appropriateness:** Ensure that the consequences are appropriate to the situation and proportional to the boundary violation.

- **Follow Through:** Enforce the consequences when necessary to uphold the integrity of the boundary and demonstrate its importance.

Ultimately, boundaries with clearly communicated and consistently enforced consequences are more likely to be respected, fostering healthier relationships and promoting self-respect and well-being. Also keep in mind that the consequences from violating your boundary are not going to be comfortable to the other person. Sometimes it may even cause a nuclear fallout level of temper tantrum. People pleasers and others who find enforcing boundaries difficult will not like this. You will feel guilty. You will want to change your mind. You will be uncomfortable. That is okay. The hardest thing you will do in this process is to accept that **You will be the villain in someone else's story regardless of how good a person you are.** It's inevitable. Being able to accept that someone, somewhere, will see you as the bad guy will make it easier to actually *be* the bad guy to people who deserve it. Remember, just because someone feels a certain way doesn't make it true. That includes the people who think you're the bad guy.

Apologies

Usually, I don't include a note about apologies when we're talking about boundaries in session because it makes clients feel like I am expecting them to apologize for something. But since you and I will never sit down together, I feel like I need to include it here. Honestly, this is a perfect place to put the apology section because at some point, healthy people (or at least minorly nice people) will apologize to you for something. Including violating your boundaries. Most people don't know what an appropriate and healthy apology actually looks like.

A healthy apology has three parts. If you do not receive all three parts, it's not really an apology. I call it the "3 A's" or "Triple A" (not to be confused with the car people, obviously).

- **Acknowledgement:** A healthy apology starts with an acknowledgement of what the person did wrong and how it affected you. A good example is – "I'm sorry that I made a comment about your outfit" or "I'm sorry. The comment I made about your ADHD was insensitive". Things like "That wasn't my intention" or "You took it the wrong way" **are not actual acknowledgement** because they put the responsibility for your response, to their statement mind you, on **you** and it doesn't belong there.
- **Apology:** This is where they say the words "I am sorry." They need to actually say those words *and just those words.* Statements like "I'm sorry you feel that way" or "I'm sorry you took it that way" **are not**

actual apologies because while they are technically saying the words but again, taking no responsibility.

- **Amends:** This is the part that most people leave out, unfortunately, and yet it is the most important. Which is a big reason why people often don't feel heard or validated when they receive an apology even when it seems like the person is sincere. Amends are a living apology, or the active form of "apology". Most often the term is used in relation to substance recovery, but it is something that is necessary in personal interactions as well. Amends are the actions the person is going to take to make sure they do not repeat the behavior. Making amends tells the person that you not only hear them but changing the behavior(s) means something to you as well as them. "I will do better about watching my language" is one example. "I will do my best to make sure that I don't make jokes like that around you again" is another. Make sure the amends are specific but not grandiose, vague, or ridiculous. "I will **never** do that again" or "Sure, I'll work on that" are not examples of amends. They are simply patronizing and trying to end the conversation without, again, taking responsibility for their actions.

So. A reminder. A healthy, appropriate apology looks a lot like this:

I didn't realize that my comment could be received that way. I hurt your feelings when I said that, and I wish that I hadn't. Even though I was joking, you found it hurtful not funny. I'm sorry for hurting your feelings. From now on, I will do my best to be more careful about the jokes I make, and I will do my best to stop making jokes like that with you.

An important note here? Don't make promises you can't keep. Saying I will *never* do something again gives the other person the expectation that it will, literally, never happen again. You're human. You will make mistakes. You may make that joke again but catch yourself in the moment and give a healthy apology for it. That doesn't mean your original apology was worthless or a lie, just that you made a mistake. Try to make sure you aren't overreaching in your attempt to make the other person feel better.

Also, keep in mind that in order to *receive* a healthy apology, you have to *give* effective communication to the person. They can't give you any part of the 3 A's if you don't tell them to stop the behavior, what exactly you're feeling, and establish a boundary with them. If you want healthy communication, you have to provide it as well.

Notes

Self-Care
Being selfish is an option and I highly recommend it.

"Self-care is not selfish. You cannot serve from an empty vessel."
-      Eleanor Brownn

Ever been on a plane? Before take-off the flight attendants go through the safety protocol. It is the same in each flight. One of those steps is what happens when the oxygen masks come down from the ceiling as a result of a change in cabin pressure. Those masks provide oxygen. The flight attendants will tell you that if you are sitting next to a child, someone who is elderly, or someone is disabled that you need to put *your* mask on first. That seems counter-intuitive for those people who like to help. But the problem with being a helper is that **You can't help someone else if you are gasping for air.** This is the "oxygen mask" scenario you will probably hear in therapy. A lot of therapists use this example to encourage self-care because no matter what the situation, it's true. You can't help anyone else if you aren't able to engage in self-care.

Self-care refers to the intentional actions and practices individuals engage in to prioritize their physical, mental, and emotional well-being. It involves taking steps to nurture and maintain one's health, reduce stress, and enhance overall quality of life. Self-care activities can vary widely and might include practices that address different aspects of well-being, such as:

- **Physical Self-Care:** This involves activities that support physical health, such as getting adequate sleep, maintaining a balanced diet, regular exercise, staying hydrated, and practicing good hygiene. This category also includes taking any medication that you might be prescribed. If you are interested in medication, I would suggest getting the genetic testing. There is now testing that you can ask for which will tell you the types of medications you should and should not be taking. It is the closest we have come to being able to do a blood test to pick a specific medication that we can guarantee will work for you. Please make sure you speak to your prescribing physician if you're interested (I highly recommend it).

- **Emotional Self-Care:** Emotional self-care focuses on managing emotions, reducing stress, and nurturing positive feelings. It may involve journaling, practicing mindfulness or meditation, engaging in hobbies, seeking therapy or counseling, or spending time with supportive friends and family.

- **Mental Self-Care:** Mental self-care involves activities that stimulate the mind, promote mental clarity, and reduce mental fatigue. This might include reading, learning new skills, puzzles, creative activities, or setting boundaries to manage stress.

- **Social Self-Care:** Social self-care involves nurturing healthy relationships and connections. This can include spending time with loved ones, joining social groups or clubs, or seeking social support when needed.

- **Spiritual Self-Care**: Spiritual self-care is about nurturing a sense of purpose, meaning, and connection to something larger than oneself. This might involve meditation, prayer, spending time in nature, or engaging in practices aligned with personal beliefs or values.

Self-care is essential for overall well-being and is not selfish or indulgent but rather a vital practice for maintaining balance and resilience in life. It's about recognizing one's own needs and taking proactive steps to meet them, which can vary for each individual. Incorporating self-care practices into daily routines can lead to improved mental health, increased energy levels, and a greater ability to manage life's challenges effectively.

Self-care looks selfish. That's because it is. Selfish, according to the Oxford Dictionary, is defined as "(of a person, action, or motive) lacking consideration for others; concerned chiefly with one's own personal profit or pleasure". When taken too far, selfishness becomes bad and can eventually lead to self-centeredness: a person "preoccupied with oneself and one's affairs". In other words, **Selfishness is putting yourself first. Self- centered is believing that everyone else should put you first as well.** The first one I encourage people to do. The second one is an example of narcissism which I never encourage people to do.

Self-care can be hard. If you are reading this in the United States, then you grew up in or at least have spent some amount of time in a capitalist society. Capitalism tells us from birth that we are only as good as what we can make to have someone else consume. And we need to *always* be creating or else we're worthless. That often (or even a lot) means that we aren't allowed to practice self-care because if you're taking care of yourself then you're not producing. The first step in self-care is to recognize that **You are more than what you produce**. You are more than what you create to be consumed. You are more than your grocery list or laundry or the dishes that 'need' to be done. You are more than the project you have to finish at work. You are more than the comfort you bring to your friends and family, even. You are a real, live, person deserving of love and care. That needs to start with you.

The second step is to **Give yourself permission**. That sounds a bit too easy, doesn't it? In theory it is pretty easy. In practice? Not so much. You inner dialogue that we talked about earlier, full of the voices of people who do not want you to take care of yourself, will argue with you. It will tell you that you "can't". There's so much to be done that comes first. If I don't take care of it, who will? The questions will pop up whenever you give yourself permission. The key is to ignore that voice and do it anyway. Don't argue with that voice because it won't work. Simply ignore it and do it anyway. "I give myself permission to be nice to myself. I give myself permission to take care of myself. I give myself permission to ignore things that are on my to-do list so I can rest." Remember, practice makes perfect. You are going to fail at this more times than you succeed and that's okay. It took you how many years to walk into therapy? Five? Ten? Twenty? It will take more than this book or one visit to a therapist for you to get really good at this. **"Baby steps" is still movement, it's just slower and takes some time to get your footing**. Progress is progress no matter how little you think you're making.

That brings me to my next point. Self-care, along with any type of emotional healing, is about **Balance, not perfection**. This way of being encapsulates the idea that striving for balance in life is more important and sustainable than pursuing an unattainable state of perfection. This concept emphasizes the importance of finding harmony and equilibrium in various aspects of life rather than seeking flawless or idealized outcomes.

Here's what "balance, not perfection" implies:

- **Acceptance of Imperfection:** It acknowledges that perfection is often unachievable and that it's okay to have imperfections or flaws. Rather than striving for flawlessness, the focus is on finding a healthy and manageable equilibrium.

- **Prioritizing Well-being:** It underscores the significance of balancing different facets of life, such as work, relationships, personal growth, and self-care, to achieve a sense of overall well-being. It emphasizes that dedicating time and energy to multiple areas is more fulfilling than fixating solely on one aspect.

- **Mindful Living:** It encourages mindfulness and self-awareness, prompting individuals to assess their priorities and make intentional choices that align with their values and needs.

- **Reducing Stress and Pressure:** Pursuing perfection can lead to undue stress, anxiety, and burnout. Embracing balance allows individuals to set realistic expectations, reducing the pressure to meet unattainable standards.

- **Flexibility and Adaptability:** Balancing different aspects of life requires flexibility and adaptability. It's about adjusting expectations and approaches to accommodate life's inevitable changes and challenges.

Ultimately, "balance, not perfection" encourages individuals to strive for a healthy and well-rounded lifestyle that acknowledges the importance of both progress and self-care. It's about finding equilibrium in a way that promotes overall happiness, fulfillment, and contentment, rather than fixating on an idealized, perfect outcome in every aspect of life. No one is perfect because no one can be. That is the nature of being human. You're going to screw up. Sometimes you're going to screw up like someone is paying you to do it. Humans have to make mistakes.

Making mistakes is an inherent part of the human experience and a fundamental aspect of learning, growth, and development. Mistakes provide valuable opportunities for learning, self-improvement, and gaining new insights. Here's why making mistakes is an essential part of life and something to embrace instead of avoiding:

- **Learning Opportunity:** Mistakes offer valuable lessons that help individuals understand what works and what doesn't. They provide a chance to gather feedback, reflect on what went wrong, and learn how to do things differently in the future.

- **Building Resilience:** Dealing with mistakes fosters resilience and the ability to bounce back from setbacks. Overcoming mistakes can build confidence, perseverance, and adaptability in facing challenges.

- **Encourages Innovation and Creativity:** Many innovations and breakthroughs have arisen from mistakes or failures. Embracing mistakes encourages experimentation, creativity, and thinking outside the box to find new solutions.

- **Humility and Self-Acceptance:** Accepting mistakes humbly acknowledges that no one is perfect. It encourages self-compassion and self-acceptance, promoting a healthier relationship with oneself.

- **Deepens Understanding:** Making mistakes helps individuals gain a deeper understanding of themselves, their capabilities, and their limitations. It allows for personal growth and self-awareness.

- **Strengthens Relationships:** Acknowledging mistakes and learning from them can improve relationships. Being open about errors and taking responsibility can build trust and understanding in personal and professional interactions.

It's important to approach mistakes with a growth mindset, viewing them as opportunities for growth and improvement rather than as failures. Embracing mistakes as part of the learning process enables individuals to move forward, armed with new knowledge and experiences that contribute to personal and professional development.

So, if mistakes are guaranteed and are necessary, then it's important to accept mistakes as part of the process. That means you can't be perfect. If you can't be perfect, then you can be balanced. Balance is not a consolation prize. It *is* the prize. Balance means you are in control of yourself, your reactions, and your feelings to such an extent that you choose where to put your energy, choose how to exercise your boundaries, and ultimately, take care of yourself effectively.

Balance is a necessary part of self-care, but it also gives you some perspective. One of the most important perspectives you can have is that **It's okay to be 'just okay'.** People who have never had to recover from anything (grief, addiction, depression, etc.), underestimate how important it is to be able to be okay. Only the people who have spent time never being able to be okay can understand this. Most of the time people are just okay. It isn't the greatest day ever but also not the worst day ever. It's just … okay. Which is, actually, okay. Satisfactory but not excellent. Content. Pick your adverb to describe it the best but whatever you pick it means the same thing: **I'm okay**. Consider what got you to this point in your life. Wouldn't it be great to be able to say that you're okay and mean it? If you are in balance, then okay is right in the middle of great and miserable and exactly where you want to be.

See? Balance!

Miserable	**Okay**	**Ecstatic**

Ultimately, boundaries exist to protect you and your peace. Have you ever heard the phrase, **Don't set yourself on fire to keep others warm**? It speaks to a person who is so out of balance that they are willing to harm themselves to take care of others. When you are always, constantly, or even consistently putting others in front of you, you are harming yourself. You won't be on your deathbed, looking back at your life, and be glad for all of the times you put others in front of you. You won't celebrate the ways in which you were taken advantage of. So do your future self a favor and put boundaries in place now so that you can enjoy your life.

Notes

Self-Esteem
How You Talk to Yourself Matters. Seriously.

"You yourself, as much as anybody in the entire universe, deserve your love and affection."
- Buddha

Self-esteem refers to a person's overall subjective sense of their own worth, value, and capabilities. It involves how individuals perceive themselves and their abilities, as well as the degree to which they value themselves as deserving of respect and acceptance. Self-esteem influences thoughts, feelings, and behaviors and plays a crucial role in various aspects of life, including mental health, relationships, and achievements.

Here are key aspects and characteristics of self-esteem:

- **Self-Worth**: Self-esteem encompasses a sense of self-worth or self-value. It involves recognizing one's inherent value as a human being, irrespective of accomplishments or external validation.

- **Self-Confidence:** A person with healthy self-esteem tends to have confidence in their abilities, skills, and decisions. They believe in themselves and their capacity to navigate challenges.

- **Self-Respect:** Individuals with healthy self-esteem tend to have self-respect, which involves treating oneself with kindness, dignity, and compassion.

- **Acceptance of Imperfection:** Healthy self-esteem involves acknowledging imperfections and mistakes without letting them negatively impact one's self-worth.

- **Resilience:** People with healthy self-esteem are often more resilient in facing setbacks or criticism. They can bounce back from failures and setbacks more effectively.

- **Autonomy:** Healthy self-esteem fosters a sense of autonomy, where individuals trust their own judgment and make decisions aligned with their values and beliefs.

- **Interactions and Relationships:** Self-esteem influences how individuals engage in relationships. Healthy self-esteem often leads to more positive and fulfilling interactions with others.

Cultivating healthy self-esteem involves self-reflection, self-acceptance, self-care, setting realistic goals, challenging negative self-talk, seeking support when needed, and practicing self-compassion. Developing a positive self-concept and valuing oneself for who they are, rather than what they do or achieve, contributes to nurturing healthy self-esteem. So why is it so difficult to just like yourself?

Part of the problem is that there are a lot of people out there who make your self-esteem their cash cow. The self-help business is a multi-million dollar one. The makeup, skin care, and hair care industries are multi-billion-dollar reasons. There is a lot of advice out there that is wrong, misleading, or even partly true but with no explanation. In the age of social media, we expect instant results so there are a lot of catchphrases out there that make it seem like it's easy when it isn't.

We might as well start with the big one. We've all heard it. Even RuPaul has a version of it (no offense to Mama Ru who I absolutely adore and hope one day to meet!!). One of the biggest myths out there about self-esteem is:

If you don't love yourself, you can't love anyone else.

Now, don't get me wrong. The statement is meant to encourage self-love and positive self-regard. It is meant to remind us that we are all loveable. Those are good things. But the message gets lost in the telling, unfortunately. It isn't that simple. Things rarely are.

So, what is so wrong about this statement? Well, when you tell someone with self-image issues that they must love themselves first you are telling them a number of things:

- What they are experiencing as love right now isn't really love.
- They are unlovable.
- They are not capable of loving someone else, which makes them inherently flawed.

For example, imagine telling your best friend, who is struggling with self-esteem issues after the birth of her first child that if she doesn't love herself then she can't love her newborn. Think about that for a second. Telling a mom who has self-esteem issues (related to being a new mom or not) that she doesn't love her own child is a horrible thing to do.

Sounds kind of ridiculous when you put it that way, right?

Yet that is what we tell people when we make that statement. That's because they do not view themselves in a positive way, that they can't experience love for someone else or for themselves. All of us are capable of love. Just because you don't love yourself does **not** in any way mean that you can't love someone else. The exact opposite is actually true. In fact, some of the most loving people I have ever met have been those who struggle with self-image and self-esteem on a regular basis. I'm not immune to issues with self-esteem either. Most of us aren't. The statement as is doesn't work so let's try to rewrite it.

If you don't love yourself, you will accept a form of love that is not only beneath you, but could actually harm you.

Not nearly as catchy, I know. The truth is rarely catchy because it is usually complicated and can't be condensed into a slogan meant to fit in a hashtag. Unfortunately, self-esteem is one of those things that take work. Sometimes it takes a lot of work. There are those of us who weren't raised in a home where our self-esteem was even noticed, much less encouraged. Most of the time people who come to therapy are already experiencing a distinct lack of self-esteem.

A lack of self-esteem means that individuals have a diminished or low sense of their own worth, value, or abilities. This can manifest in various ways and may significantly impact an individual's thoughts, feelings, behaviors, and overall well-being. Here are some characteristics and effects associated with a lack of self-esteem:

- **Negative Self-Image:** Individuals with low self-esteem often have a negative perception of themselves. They may focus on perceived flaws, shortcomings, or mistakes, leading to self-criticism and self-doubt.

- **Self-Doubt and Insecurity:** A lack of self-esteem can result in constant self-doubt and feelings of insecurity. Individuals may question their abilities, judgment, or worthiness, leading to hesitancy in decision-making and reluctance to take on challenges.

- **Fear of Rejection or Failure:** People with low self-esteem may fear rejection or failure excessively. This fear can prevent them from pursuing opportunities or forming meaningful connections due to the anticipation of criticism or disappointment.

- **Perfectionism:** Some individuals with low self-esteem might strive for perfection as a way to gain external validation or cover up their feelings of inadequacy. This pursuit of perfection can be exhausting and lead to increased stress.

- **Avoidance of Risks:** Due to fear of failure or criticism, individuals with low self-esteem might avoid taking risks or trying new things, limiting their growth and opportunities for personal development.

- **Impact on Relationships:** Low self-esteem can affect relationships, leading to difficulties in forming healthy connections. It might result in seeking excessive approval from others or tolerating unhealthy relationships due to a lack of self-worth.

- **Emotional Impact:** Low self-esteem can contribute to feelings of sadness, anxiety, or depression. It can also affect mental health, leading to increased stress and decreased resilience in facing life's challenges.

Addressing a lack of self-esteem involves self-reflection, self-compassion, and taking steps to improve self-perception and confidence. Seeking support from a therapist, counselor, or support group can be beneficial in developing self-awareness, challenging negative beliefs, and learning healthy coping strategies. Building self-esteem is a gradual process that involves self-acceptance, nurturing strengths, setting realistic goals, and practicing self-care and self-compassion.

There is one further thing to consider when it comes to self-esteem. If you have a history of trauma including abuse, bullying, and trauma, I need you to pay attention to this next part. It is understandable that those experiences caused you to have low self-esteem. That low self-esteem includes a narrative that was created by your brain as a result of the trauma. I want you to ask yourself the following questions:

- Would you talk to a loved one the way you talk to yourself?
- Does talking to yourself this way feel good?

- Does talking to yourself this way make things better?

If the answer is no to all three of those questions (and it should be, by the way), then **You have become your own primary abuser.** You've picked up where they left off. Shocking, isn't it? I hope so. Because your low self-esteem, and all of the ugly things you say to yourself, means that you have now taken over for all of the people who have hurt you to do it yourself.

Now, it's time to take a breath. Before you start the shame spiral (that we both know is coming), let's retreat to your logical brain for a minute. The statement is not a weapon to beat yourself up with. No one taught you how to be kind to yourself. No one taught you that life isn't supposed to be this painful. If all you've ever known is pain, you can't know how to take care of yourself. That is why therapy is so important. It can teach you how to navigate the thoughts as well as help you heal from the trauma.

Jean Piaget, a pioneering psychologist in the field of child development, proposed a theory outlining four stages of cognitive development that children progress through as they grow. According to Piaget, children's understanding of the world evolves through these distinct stages, each characterized by specific cognitive abilities and ways of thinking. What does this have to do with you? Read on.

In the stage of development known as the preoperational stage (which typically occurs roughly from ages 2 to 7), children are advancing in language development and symbolic thinking, but they still struggle with logical reasoning and understanding cause-and-effect relationships in a sophisticated manner. Instead, at this stage, children demonstrate egocentric thinking, where they perceive the world primarily from their perspective and have difficulty understanding others' viewpoints fully. They might lack a comprehensive understanding of complex situations and might tend to attribute events to themselves, especially in situations involving conflict or distress.

When children experience stress, conflict, or challenges within their environment (such as parental conflict, family changes, or school issues), they might attribute these problems to themselves due to their limited understanding of cause and effect. This can lead to feelings of guilt, self-blame, or a belief that they caused the problem. In very simple words, when a child experiences a trauma, they blame themselves, **each and every time,** because they believe that the world revolves around them. Parents get divorced? Your fault. Teacher in a bad mood? Your fault. Don't have any friends? Absolutely your fault. Everything is always your fault.

Before the age of 10, children see the world in black and white terms – if good things are happening that must mean I'm good which means if bad things are happening that must mean I'm bad. Despite maturing as they get older, gaining the understanding that people have their own identities, that childhood belief sticks with you wherever you go for the rest of your life. Unless you go to therapy that is. That internal belief makes you act a certain way. Specifically, you believe that you cause bad things to happen, so you're not surprised when they do, and you don't do anything to avoid them. You're not surprised when your romantic partner treats you badly, because hasn't everyone? You walk around believing to your very core that you are worthless (and, unfortunately, you find people to treat you that way when in that mindset which causes a vicious cycle). But considering what happened to you when you were a kid, it makes sense. Take a kid who will blame themselves for anything bad, add in traumatic experiences, and you have the recipe for disaster. Inner child work is something I recommend you bring up with your therapist, especially if you had a traumatic childhood.

It's important to note that self-esteem is not fixed and can fluctuate based on experiences, life events, and internal thoughts. Both internal factors (such as self-talk, beliefs, and perceptions) and external factors (feedback from others, societal influences) can impact self-esteem. Self-esteem is also a positive side effect of healing. The more you heal, the more you like yourself and like eventually leads to love.

Notes

Healing
Just Because it Hurts, Doesn't Mean it Isn't Working

"The privilege of a lifetime is to become who you truly are."
- Carl Jung

Healing hurts. The things that caused you pain before will cause you pain again when you remember it and speak it out loud. Therapy will be painful, but that doesn't mean it has to be torture. Effective therapy will be painful but gentle. Healing emotional wounds is a gradual and individualized process that involves acknowledging, understanding, and working through painful experiences or traumas that have caused emotional distress. Here are steps and strategies that can help in the healing process:

- **Acknowledgment and Acceptance:** Acknowledge and accept your emotions and the wounds you carry. Accepting that emotional pain exists and deserves attention is the first step toward healing.

- **Self-Compassion:** Practice self-compassion by being kind and understanding toward yourself. Treat yourself with the same empathy and care you would offer to a friend facing a similar situation.

- **Seek Support:** Reach out to trusted friends, family, or a therapist for support. Talking about your feelings and experiences with someone you trust can provide validation, comfort, and perspective.

- **Explore Your Emotions:** Allow yourself to experience and express your emotions in a healthy way. Journaling, art, music, or mindfulness are some practices that can help you explore and process your feelings.

- **Set Boundaries:** Establish boundaries that protect your emotional well-being. This might involve limiting contact with people or situations that trigger emotional distress.

- **Mindfulness and Self-Care:** Engage in mindfulness practices, meditation, or relaxation techniques to ground yourself and reduce stress. Prioritize self-care activities that nurture your physical, mental, and emotional health.

- **Professional Help:** Consider seeking therapy or counseling to work through deeper emotional wounds. Therapists can provide tools, guidance, and support tailored to your specific needs. If necessary, be willing to explore medication options with a psychiatrist as well.

- **Empowerment and Growth:** Focus on personal growth and empowerment. Engage in activities or hobbies that make you feel confident, strong, and connected to your inner strengths and values.

- **Patience and Time**: Healing emotional wounds takes time. Be patient and gentle with yourself throughout the process. Understand that healing is not linear and may involve setbacks or difficult moments.

See where I've been going this whole time? All of the things we've already discussed are key factors in healing. Remember, those factors and everyone's healing journey is unique. What works for one person may not work for another. It's essential (I know I keep saying it but there are so many things essential to therapeutic work!) to find approaches that resonate with you and support your emotional healing process. Be compassionate toward yourself and celebrate your progress, no matter how small it may seem. Healing emotional wounds is a significant step toward greater emotional well-being and resilience.

When you are in the midst of your healing journey, you'll discover that **Everything is temporary**. Emotions are temporary. Bad days are temporary. Jerk bosses are temporary. Sometimes love is. You name it, and it's temporary. Nothing lasts forever. Not even pain. That is the first hope offered to those who are working on themselves: Your pain is temporary. People often say, "This too shall pass" to indicate that hard times are temporary. That's true but it doesn't tell the full story. I prefer my grandfather's version: "This too shall pass. Like a god damn kidney stone, but it'll pass."

Now that we know it is temporary, let's go over something that often trips people up: the belief in closure. I hate to break it to you, but **Closure is a myth.** I know, I know. There are so many people out there who would argue with me including some authors who make a lot of money talking about it. Someone, somewhere, is about to send me hate mail because of this. But it's true. Closure is a myth. The idea of closure is often considered in the context of finding resolution or a sense of completeness after experiencing loss, trauma, or the end of a relationship. There are a few problems with that way of thinking though.

First, emotional healing and recovery after a significant event vary from person to person. Some experiences, such as the loss of a loved one, trauma, or the end of a relationship, can have a lasting emotional impact. Seeking closure will not erase that pain, only prolong it because there is no finish line. Second, closure implies a sense of finality or resolution. However, in many cases, situations don't have a clear endpoint due to circumstances beyond one's control making closure as we know it impossible.

The biggest reason it is a myth: Closure relies on someone else healing your hurt. Except they can't. No one has the ability to heal anyone but themselves. The person that hurt you can never say or do anything that will erase the damage they caused. Even if they miraculously say the exact thing that you have always wanted them to say, there will be no proof that they mean it. You'll have no idea if they are lying to you or not. If you can't trust someone, you can't heal from their actions. Even if they did mean it, you will always wonder why now? When did they figure it out and why after so long? Why couldn't they just not hurt you? There will never be an answer to those types of questions. At least not an answer good enough to make the harm seem justified. Then the cycle starts all over again.

Instead of seeking closure, focusing on healing, self-care, and personal growth can be more beneficial.

Acknowledging and processing emotions is crucial during the healing process. Closure should instead be redefined as an ongoing process of acceptance, adaptation, and growth rather than a specific endpoint. It involves learning to live with unanswered questions and finding peace despite unresolved issues. The process of healing, self-reflection, and finding meaning in one's experiences can contribute to emotional well-being. It's important to allow oneself the time and space needed to heal and come to terms with difficult circumstances, even if closure in its traditional sense doesn't exist.

With that out of the way, let's dive into the issue of forgiveness and healing. You've heard that "forgiveness is divine" and "not forgiving someone is like drinking poison and waiting for them to die" and other utter nonsense. If my disdain isn't obvious, let me be crystal clear: **You don't need to forgive the people who hurt you in order to find healing**. This one I am definitely going to get hate mail for. I'm okay with that because it's true. Seriously.

Forgiveness of those who have hurt you is a spiritual and not psychological principle. While psychology has studied forgiveness and its effect on people's well-being, the act of forgiveness is one created by religion. If your religion requires or encourages forgiveness and that is important to you, then knock yourself out. I just don't want you to think that if you can't forgive the person or people who have harmed you, that there is something wrong with you or you will never find peace. That is just not true. There are no psychological principles requiring forgiveness for healing except one: Forgiving yourself.

Forgiving oneself can be a challenging but important process in achieving self-acceptance, healing, and personal growth. Here are steps and strategies that may help you in finding that forgiveness:

- **Acknowledge and Accept Responsibility**: Take responsibility for your actions or mistakes without blaming yourself excessively. Only take on what belongs to you and discard the rest. Acknowledge what happened and its impact while recognizing that everyone makes mistakes.

- **Understand the Circumstances:** Understand the context and circumstances that led to the mistake or action. Consider factors such as stress, emotions, or external influences that might have contributed. Be realistic instead of just blaming yourself.

- **Learn from the Experience:** Reflect on the situation and the lessons it offers. What can you learn from this experience? How can you prevent similar situations in the future?

- **Practice Self-Compassion:** Treat yourself with kindness and understanding. Practice self-compassion by offering yourself the same empathy and support you would offer to a friend facing a similar situation.

- **Let Go of Perfectionism:** Understand that nobody is perfect. Embrace your imperfections and mistakes as part of the human experience. Striving for improvement is admirable, but expecting perfection can be unrealistic and harmful.

- **Release Guilt and Shame:** Understand the difference between healthy remorse and excessive guilt or shame. Healthy remorse motivates positive change, while excessive guilt can be detrimental to your well-being.

- **Challenge Negative Self-Talk**: Be aware of negative self-talk or self-criticism. Challenge negative thoughts and replace them with more realistic and compassionate self-talk.

- **Practice Mindfulness and Self-Care**: Engage in mindfulness practices or self-care activities that help ground you in the present moment and reduce stress. Taking care of yourself physically, mentally, and emotionally is crucial in the forgiveness process.

- **Seek Support**: Talk to a trusted friend, family member, counselor, or therapist if you're struggling to forgive yourself. Sharing your feelings and seeking guidance can offer valuable support.

- **Give Yourself Time**: Forgiving oneself is a process that takes time. Be patient with yourself and understand that healing and self-forgiveness often occur gradually.

Remember, forgiving yourself doesn't mean forgetting or dismissing the impact of your actions. It's about acknowledging, learning, and growing from your experiences while releasing yourself from the burden of excessive self-blame and guilt. If you choose to forgive the person, then you are making it an active choice to do so, not an obligation. Self-forgiveness is an important step toward self-compassion, healing, and personal well-being.

Part of forgiving yourself means changing your perspective on things you've always believed to be true. The first of these is: **There is no such thing as letting go of trauma**. So, stop telling yourself and others that you just have to "let it go". Your emotional trauma is not baggage. It isn't like you've packed your memories into suitcases that you can put down on the side of the road and drive away. Saying that insinuates, even subconsciously, that you have control over holding onto the trauma and so if you can't just "let it go" then there is something wrong with. This implies responsibility which slides really easily into blame. You do not have control over your trauma. You are not choosing to keep it with you. There is no reason to blame yourself or hold yourself accountable. Allowing yourself to change your perspective on this will be a huge leap forward in your healing.

Now let's take a look at the definition of insanity. You've heard it. I've heard it. Everyone has heard it.

The definition of insanity is doing the same thing over and over again while expecting different results.

This saying irritates me when I hear it for a few reasons. First, that is definitely not insanity. If you have ever encountered real mental illness, you wouldn't be so flippant with that term. Second, no one who is participating in a toxic or dysfunctional relationship wants to be harmed. Finally, this phrase tells people who are stuck in damaging cycles the following:

- Their participation in this cycle is one of active choice.
- They know the situation won't change, and still participate.
- They are crazy.

No one wants to be told they are crazy or that they are choosing trauma. People don't stay in cycles because they're insane. They stay because they hope for change, but they don't know how to get it. So, one way of rewriting the phrase is:

The definition of **toxic hope** *is doing the same thing over and over again while expecting different results.*

However, there is one way in particular that I believe this statement should be written.

The definition of **intergenerational trauma** *is doing the same thing over and over again while expecting different results.*

Your parents could not teach you what they were not taught by their parents who were not taught by theirs and so on. Families like this tend to express statements like, "It was good enough for me so it's good enough for my kids", "I got hit/spanked/neglected and I turned out just fine!", "We don't talk about family business outside of the family", and my personal favorite, "Therapy isn't real and doesn't help people." All of those statements and their derivatives amount to generations of people who refused to do the work to heal themselves before having children and passing on their trauma. They are the same people who believe "You just have to work harder" for anything. However, trying doesn't guarantee success so that statement puts the blame and responsibility firmly on the shoulders of the person who had been victimized. Not knowing how to ask for help when things go wrong and believing that you just have to try hard enough to overcome or change things keeps people trapped in cycles that they don't even know they can escape, much less how to do so. These cliches have a habit of making people feel responsible for things that are beyond their control. Changing your perspective on this and other outdated cliches is a step in the right direction of healing.

Spoon Theory

Speaking of perspective, our next stop is the Spoon Theory. The Spoon Theory is a metaphor used to explain the limited energy and abilities of individuals with chronic illnesses, mental health issues, and disabilities. This theory was created by Christine Miserandino, who used spoons as a tangible representation of the finite amount of energy or resources that someone with a chronic illness possesses each day.

In a conversation with her friend, Miserandino used spoons from a nearby table to illustrate how she managed her energy throughout the day. She handed her friend a few spoons and explained that each spoon represented a unit of energy required to complete a task. People with chronic illnesses, mental health issues, or disabilities often have a limited number of "spoons" or units of energy available for their daily activities. Simple tasks might cost one or more spoons, and once these "spoons" are used up, a person might not have the energy to complete additional tasks for the day.

The Spoon Theory serves as a way to explain to others the concept of limited energy and the necessity of making choices and prioritizing tasks. It helps individuals with chronic illnesses or disabilities convey the challenges they face in managing their energy and the importance of pacing themselves to avoid exhaustion or flare-ups.

By using the Spoon Theory, individuals can better communicate the impact of their condition their on daily life, fostering understanding and empathy from friends, family, and others who may not have experienced similar limitations. It has become a powerful tool for building awareness and promoting understanding of the struggles faced by those with chronic illnesses or disabilities in managing their energy and daily activities.

So, why bring this up in the section on healing? Because being realistic about what you are capable of, with what resources you have available, is the cornerstone of healing. It also ties into boundaries. Being able to effectively measure your energy levels means that you know when to say no to something in order to take care of yourself (brought it full circle! Everything connects.). When you start to feel better, you will become more dedicated to not only measuring your spoons but protecting your newfound peace and wellness. That will eventually become your new state of mind and then you'll know you've healed.

Crying

I decided to end this section with one of the most misunderstood behaviors that humans engage in: crying. I can't tell you the number of times over the years that I have had clients who have issues with crying. I've heard every excuse you can imagine for why people hate it, avoid it, won't do it in front of other people: if someone has said it, I've probably heard it. One of my sarcastically favorite ones is the notorious "Crying makes you WEAK". There is a surprising amount of people in the world who intensely dislike what is a *bodily function*. Imagine if people hated blinking with that much fervor. It's a bit weird, honestly, when you break it down like that. Right?!

And yet, repeatedly over the years, I have had to explain why crying is not shameful but necessary. Crying is a complex emotional and physiological process that can have healing effects on an individual's mental and emotional well-being. While the direct "healing" effects of crying can vary between individuals and situations, scientific research and studies have suggested several potential ways in which crying may contribute to emotional and psychological well-being:

- **Release of Stress Hormones:** Crying can trigger the release of stress hormones, such as adrenocorticotropic hormone (ACTH) and endorphins. This release may help reduce stress and alleviate tension, leading to a sense of relief and relaxation.

- **Mood Improvement**: Tears contain stress hormones and toxins, and crying can help expel these substances from the body. This release may contribute to mood improvement and a sense of emotional cleansing.

- **Emotional Regulation:** Crying can act as a natural emotional regulator. It helps individuals process and express intense emotions, potentially leading to a reduction in emotional distress.

- **Pain Relief:** Some studies suggest that crying may trigger the release of endorphins, the body's natural painkillers, which can contribute to a temporary reduction in physical pain and an overall sense of well-being.

- **Cathartic Effect:** Crying often accompanies moments of deep emotional processing and catharsis. It allows individuals to express and confront difficult emotions, leading to a sense of emotional release and resolution.

- **Social Connection:** Tears can serve as a non-verbal form of communication, signaling distress or a need for support. This can facilitate social connection and empathy, leading to comfort and support from others.

While these scientific explanations shed light on the potential benefits of crying, it's important to note that the healing effects of crying can vary widely among individuals. The interpretation and experience of crying depend on various factors, including personal circumstances, cultural influences, and individual emotional responses.

The act of crying alone may not solve underlying problems or completely alleviate emotional distress. Seeking professional support, such as therapy or counseling, can complement the emotional release provided by crying, helping individuals address and work through underlying issues contributing to their emotional distress.

Here's why crying in therapy can be significant:

- **Emotional Release:** Crying allows for the release of pent-up emotions. It can be a way to express and process feelings that may have been suppressed or difficult to articulate verbally.

- **Cathartic Effect:** Crying can have a cathartic effect, providing a sense of relief and emotional cleansing. It can help alleviate stress, anxiety, or feelings of overwhelm.

- **Deep Emotional Exploration:** Tears often accompany moments of deep emotional exploration. They can signal that a person is touching upon sensitive, meaningful, or unresolved issues during therapy.

- **Non-Verbal Expression:** Sometimes, emotions are difficult to put into words. Crying serves as a non-verbal form of expression, communicating feelings that may be challenging to verbalize.

- **Release of Tension:** Crying can help release physical tension and stress. It can signal the body's way of releasing built-up emotional and physical tension.

- **Increased Emotional Connection:** For some individuals, crying in therapy can deepen the therapeutic relationship and enhance trust between the client and therapist.

It's essential to recognize that everyone's emotional expression is unique, and not everyone may cry during therapy sessions. The goal of therapy is not to force tears but to create a safe and supportive environment where individuals feel comfortable expressing their emotions in whatever way feels natural to them. Therapists are trained to provide a compassionate and non-judgmental space where clients can express themselves freely, whether through tears, words, or other forms of emotional expression. Ultimately, the presence or absence of tears in therapy doesn't determine the effectiveness of the session but rather the willingness to engage authentically with one's emotions and experiences.

On a side note, if you want to see something really cool (in my opinion), do a Google search for "different tears under a microscope" or "microscopic structures of human tears". Hit the "Images" tab and check out the results!

Notes

Conclusion
Are we there yet?

"The good life is a process, not a state of being. It is a direction, not a destination."
\- Carl Rogers

Dear Reader,

As I close this book, I struggle to identify exactly what this offers to you. The intent was simple: to shine a light on the therapeutic journey, sprinkled with humor and relatable anecdotes. But did I do that? I hope so. I'm sure I'll hear about it if I didn't!

The truth is the automobile accident I mentioned in the introduction caused a hemorrhagic stroke. That stroke ended my career overnight (and only 2 years after getting my PhD). When I was informing my clients of my forced retirement, many of them asked me to write a book so that they could remember the things we've discussed over the years. At a minimum, this book is for them and because of them. Without my clients I wouldn't be who I am today. I also wouldn't have so much material to share! At the end of the day, I simply hope that this book, along with the years I spent as a therapist, will have a positive impact on people long after I am gone.

Throughout these pages, I've aimed to destigmatize therapy a bit, as well as normalizing the pursuit of self-improvement through healing. It's not merely about "fixing" something; it's about embracing the human experience in all its complexities. If it ain't broke, don't fix it as they say. And you're not broken.

After reading this, I encourage you to reflect on your own therapy experiences if you have them. If you do not have experience in therapy yet, ask yourself what has been holding you back from scheduling an appointment. Embrace the imperfections and celebrate your progress—no matter how small. Remember, "baby steps" is still movement and no matter where you are in the process, I know you are doing great.

The journey towards personal growth is ongoing. It is a marathon, not a sprint. Embrace each step, find the joy in the process, and continue nurturing your emotional well-being. And always, always remember to laugh. It makes life worth living and the hurt a little less.

May your journey be filled with laughter, self-discovery, and an abundance of personal growth.

Dr. Marie

One More Thing!

Okay, maybe more than one.

Please note that the paperback copy of this work has lines for notes when the Kindle Version does not.

Below are the works Dr. Marie has created in this series as well as her contact information.

Things My Therapist Said (this one)

Things My Therapist Said: The Workbook (Amazon)

Things My Therapist Said: The Flip Book (on website only, forthcoming)

Things My Therapist Said: The Big Book of Exercises (forthcoming)

www.voyagerhealthservices.net